Isabella

From Auschwitz
to Freedom

Isabella Leitner
and Irving A. Leitner

ANCHOR BOOKS
DOUBLEDAY
New York London Toronto Sydney Auckland

AN ANCHOR BOOK
PUBLISHED BY DOUBLEDAY
a division of Bantam Doubleday Dell Publishing Group, Inc.
1540 Broadway, New York, New York 10036

ANCHOR BOOKS, DOUBLEDAY, and the portrayal of an anchor are
trademarks of Doubleday, a division of Bantam Doubleday Dell
Publishing Group, Inc.

Library of Congress Cataloging-in-Publication Data

Leitner, Isabella.
Isabella: from Auschwitz to freedom/by Isabella Leitner and
Irving A. Leitner.—1st Anchor Books ed.
p.   cm.
Merges and re-works the author's Fragments of Isabella,
and Saving the fragments.
1. Leitner, Isabella. 2. Holocaust, Jewish (1939–1945)—Personal
narratives. 3. Auschwitz (Poland: Concentration camp)
4. Holocaust survivors—United States—Biography. 5. Jews—United States—
Biography. I. Leitner, Irving A. II. Leitner, Isabella.
Fragments of Isabella. III. Leitner, Isabella. Saving the
fragments. IV. Title.
D804.3.L453   1994
940.53'18—dc20   93-47892
CIP

For Tobe, Mendel, Sadie, Hyman, Cipi, and Potyo

The recall was painful.
My husband tiptoed around
me with deep, delicate concern.
This book belongs to him.

ISABELLA

In honor of the
United States Holocaust Memorial Museum:

"To Save Your Children, You Must Remember Ours."

You don't die of anything
except death.
Suffering doesn't kill you.
Only death.

May 31, 1944

A half century ago
Hitler said I must be gassed
or burned alive
in the crematoriums of Auschwitz.
I was brought there in a sealed cattle car
and was greeted by a doctor whose business
was murder, not healing.
His name was Dr. Josef Mengele.
With a slight whistling sound,
and a flick of his finger,
he ordered me to live for a while
in the annihilation camp—Lager C—
gateway to skeletonship and ashes.
Strange how his outer appearance
resembled that of a man.
Do beasts wear elegant uniforms?
I alighted from the traveling coffin;
chaos and shrieks were everywhere—
desperate sounds of *Mama, Papa, Papa, Mama,*
Pa-pa, Ma-ma, Cipi, Aaron, Eva, Samuel, Ma-ma!
commingled with sounds of barking dogs
   and barking SS

ordering us rotten Jews not to panic but to
behave like human beings.
It was a Wednesday afternoon, the last day
of a beauteous month called May.
Children's deafening, bloodcurdling cries
soared heavenward from the hell pits of fire,
where macabre flames danced in the foul-smelling
stench of spring air, for the crematoriums alone
could not accommodate the huge cargo of humans
who must be burned that afternoon.
My eyes turned skyward in search of a patch of sky,
but all I could see was a kingdom of hell
bathed in the darkest of swirling, charcoal gray smoke,
and my nostrils were saturated with the scent of
burning flesh, and the scent was that of my mother,
my sister, and each passenger's kin,
and half a century later, I am unable to inhale
air only, for the scent of singed human flesh
is permanently lodged in my nostrils.
I do not look different from other people,
but tread gently as you pass me by, for my skull
is inhabited by phantoms in the dark of night
and sights and sounds in the light of day
that are different from those that live in souls
who were not in Auschwitz a half century ago.

The sun made a desperate effort to shine on the last day of May in 1944. The sun is warm in May. It heals. But even the heavens were helpless on that day. A force so evil ruled heaven and earth that it altered the natural order of the universe, and the heart of my mother was floating in the smoke-filled sky of Auschwitz. I have tried to rub the smoke out of my vision for decades, but my eyes are still burning, Mother.

For years, my younger sister did not allow me to use her real name in print. I now have her permission to do so. In the original publication of *Fragments of Isabella* and *Saving the Fragments*, I called her "Rachel." Rachel's true name is Regina.

Contents

Introduction

ON MAY 8, 1945, the very day World War II ended in Europe, the U.S. merchant marine ship SS *Brand Whitlock,* after nearly five weeks at sea, sailed into the sunlit harbor of Newport News, Virginia. Two days later, in Baltimore, Maryland, the ship discharged an extraordinary cargo, the very first survivors of Auschwitz, my two sisters and myself. In our battered beings we carried the charred souls of millions of innocent children, women, and men.

This America, this best of all countries, put its healing arms around me. Still, the pain would not go away.

To get some relief, I needed to talk. But to whom? My sisters? They knew everything. To those who were not there? They were unable to understand anything. In those early days—even now—Auschwitz was—and is—unfathomable. Naive questions only increased my frustration. Yet I had to talk. I just had to.

I began to "speak" on little scraps of paper in my native tongue, Hungarian, using a pencil. When the images of Auschwitz forced themselves to the threshold of my memory, I would write wherever I happened to be—on the bus, in the kitchen, in the bathroom, in the owlish hours of night, in the bright light of day. Then, as I felt a bit better, I would discard the memories in the trash—until one day, when a mysterious sense of history silently whispered in my heart to save them, to try to leave a piece of my soul behind, for whatever the future might be.

Finally, I began to write my first book, *Fragments of Isabella: A Memoir of Auschwitz*. Years had passed, and because I was afraid to rely on my memory only, I reached for my box of faded shreds of paper, and began to translate them. Nearly all the words found their way into the manuscript. How glad I was, for originally they had been written in the immediate aftermath of the war and carried the weight of authenticity.

Fragments of Isabella: A Memoir of Auschwitz was published in 1978.

Then, several years later, the need to tell more of my story surfaced again, and a second book was born.

Saving the Fragments: From Auschwitz to New York was published in 1985.

Now, in the waning years of my life, to see the two books become one—that is as it should be—gives me a measure of peace.

ISABELLA LEITNER
New York, 1993

BOOK ONE
AUSCHWITZ

YESTERDAY, what happened yesterday? Did you go to the movies? Did you have a date? What did he say? That he loves you? Did you see the new Garbo film? She was wearing a stunning cape. Her hair, I thought, was completely different and very becoming. Have you seen it? No? I haven't. Yesterday . . . yesterday, May 29, 1944, we were deported. . . .

Are the American girls really going to the movies? Do they have dates? Men tell them they love them, true or not. Their hair is long and blonde, high in the front and low in the back, like this and like that, and they are beautiful and homely. Their clothes are light in the summer and they wear fur in the winter—they mustn't catch cold. They wear stockings, ride in automobiles, wear wristwatches and necklaces, and they are colorful and perfumed. They are healthy. They are living. Incredible!

Was it only a year ago? Or a century? . . . Our heads are shaved. We look like neither boys nor girls. We haven't menstruated for a long time. We have diarrhea. No, not diarrhea—typhus. Summer and winter we have but one type of clothing. Its name is "rag." Not an inch of it without a hole. Our shoulders are exposed. The rain is pouring on our skeletal bodies. The lice are having an orgy in our armpits, their favorite spots. Their blood-sucking, the irritation, their busy scurrying, give the illusion of warmth. We're hot at least under our armpits, while our bodies are shivering.

MAY 28, 1944— MORNING

IT IS SUNDAY, May 28, my birthday, and I am celebrating, packing for the big journey, mumbling to myself with bitter laughter—tomorrow is deportation. The laughter is too bitter, the body too tired, the soul trying to still the infinite rage. My skull seems to be ripping apart, trying to organize, to comprehend what cannot be comprehended. Deportation? What is it like?

A youthful SS man, with the authority, might, and terror of the whole German army in his voice, has just informed us that we are to rise at 4 A.M. sharp for the journey. Anyone not up at 4 A.M. will get a *Kugel* (bullet).

A bullet simply for not getting up? What is happening here? The ghetto suddenly seems beautiful. I want to celebrate my birthday for all the days to come in this heaven. God, please let us stay here. Show us you are merciful. If my senses are accurate, this is the last paradise we will ever know. Please let us stay in this heavenly hell forever. Amen. We want nothing—nothing, just to stay in the ghetto. We are not crowded, we are not hungry, we are not miserable, we are happy. Dear ghetto, we love you; don't let us leave. We were wrong to complain, we never meant it.

We're tightly packed in the ghetto, but that must be a fine way to live in comparison to deportation. Did God take leave of his senses? Something terrible is coming. Or is it only me? Am I mad? There are seven of us in nine feet of space. Let them put fourteen together, twenty-eight. We will sleep on top of each other. We will get up at 3 A.M.—not 4—stand in line for ten hours. Anything. Anything. Just let our family stay together. Together we will endure death. Even life.

MAY 28, 1944—
AFTERNOON

WE ARE NO LONGER being guarded only by the Hungarian gendarmes. That duty has been taken over by the SS, for tomorrow we are to be transported. From now on, the SS are to be the visible bosses.

Before this day, Admiral Horthy's gendarmes were the front men. Now they are what they always had been—the lackeys. Ever since childhood, I remembered them with terror in my heart. They were brutal, vicious—and anti-Semitic. Ordinary policemen, by comparison, are gentle and kind. But now, for the first time, the SS are to take charge.

My mother looks at me, her birthday baby. My mother's face, her eyes, cannot be described. From here on she keeps smiling. Her smile is full of pain. She knows that for her there is nothing beyond this. And she keeps smiling at me, and I cannot stand it. I am silently pleading with her: "Stop smiling." I gaze at her tenderly and smile back.

I would love to tell her that she should trust me, that I will live, endure. And she trusts me, but she doesn't trust the Germans. She keeps smiling, and it is driving me mad, because deep inside I know she knows. I keep hearing her oft-made comment: "Hitler will lose the war, but he'll win against the Jews."

And now an SS man is here, spick-and-span, with a dog, a silver pistol, and a whip. And he is all of sixteen years old. On his list appears the name of every Jew in the ghetto. The streets are bulging with Jews, because Kisvárda, a little town, has to accommodate all the Jews of the neighboring villages. The SS do not have to pluck out every Jew from every hamlet. That work has already been done by the gendarmes. The Jews are now here. All the SS have to do is to send them on their way.

The Jews are lined up in the streets. And now the sixteen-year-old SS begins to read the names. Those called form a group opposite us. "Teresa Katz," he calls—my mother. She steps forward. My brother, my sisters, and I watch her closely. (My father is in America trying to obtain immigration papers for his wife and children, trying to save them before Hitler devours them.) My mother heads toward the group.

Now the SS man moves toward my mother. He raises his whip and, for no reason at all, lashes out at her.

Philip, my eighteen-year-old brother, the only man left in the family, starts to leap forward to tear the sixteen-year-old SS apart. And we, the sisters—don't we want to do the same?

But suddenly reality stares at us with all its madness. My mother's blood will flow right here in front of our eyes. Philip will be butchered. We are unarmed, untrained. We are children. Our weapon might be a shoelace or a belt. Besides, we don't know how to kill. The SS whistle will bring forth all the other SS and gendarmes, and they will not be merciful enough to kill the entire ghetto—only enough to create a pool of blood. All of this flashes before us with crystal clarity. Our mother's blood must not be shed right here, right now, in front of our very eyes. Our brother must not be butchered.

And so my sister Chicha and I, standing next to Philip, step on his feet and hold his arms as hard as we can. And Philip's eyes flash in disbelief. We are all anguished. But we are all still alive.

MY FATHER

MY FATHER left Hungary for America. He left in trepidation, leaving his wife and six children behind. He left so he might save his family. He spent all his energies, all his love, banging on the doors of the authorities: "Give me immigration papers for my precious seven, so they can come here and live. Don't let them be murdered."

And they gave him the papers, *finally.*

But the clock ticked faster than the hands of bureaucracy moved. We received the necessary documents with instructions to be at the American consulate in Budapest on a certain Monday morning. My mother, Chicha, and I arrived in Budapest on Sunday. We were good and early, for on Monday morning we had an appointment with life!

We were at a friend's house, chatting happily about the appointment, listening to music on the radio. There was a sudden interruption. The music stopped.

There was no appointment at the American consulate on Monday morning. It was December 8, 1941. Hungary had declared war against the United States.

The desperate father is again banging on the doors of the authorities: "Give me papers for Palestine [now Israel], so that my precious seven might live."

And they gave him the papers, *finally*.

And we received them . . . four weeks after Hitler had occupied Hungary. They could be framed . . . or used for toilet paper. I don't remember what we did with them.

Many years later, as you lay dying, Father, were you still tormented? Did you still think you had not done everything possible?

You tried, Father. You tried.

MAIN STREET, HUNGARY

KISVÁRDA was a small town in Hungary with a population of only twenty thousand. Yet it stands out in my memory as a very sophisticated "city" with visiting opera and theater companies, masquerade balls for the rich, cafés in which to while away the time trying to sound clever and worldly, auto racing, and horse racing. Barons, princes, and rich landowners, with their high-class manners and designer clothes, pranced around town in their fancy carriages. These aristocrats put their stamp on the town.

Main Street in Kisvárda (St. Laszlo Utca), I remember, smelled of French perfumes when I used to accompany my mother to the marketplace. The aroma would fill my nostrils as I'd watch my mother feel the force-fed geese to see if they were fat enough to nourish her six growing children—her bright, handsome, sensitive kids who would one day go out into the world well prepared by a mother whose intelligence and enlightenment were legendary and whose social conscience earned her my title "the poor man's Mrs. Roosevelt."

An avid reader, my mother marched her six kids off to the library every Friday to borrow the maximum number of books allowed to us, which she herself would devour before they had to be returned. And when my mother would buy fish for the Sabbath or holidays, she was incapable of throwing away the newspapers the fish were wrapped in before reading the smelly sheets first.

And I remember Teca, the gypsy, who used to come around to cast her sad eyes at my mother every day. Her source of sadness was always the same: "My children are hungry, Ma'am." And "Ma'am" would invariably fill Teca's potato sack with whatever she could spare. And anyone happening by at mealtime would automatically be invited to dine with us. "There will be enough. I'll put a little more water in the soup."

But mostly I remember the conversations my mother used to have with the many adults who came to visit us from other parts of Europe—business people, friends, relatives. The six kids stood around drinking in those very big words, those very big subjects—politics, art, books, and always *man's inhumanity to man.* Sometimes I was resentful. Must she care about everyone in this world? Look at me! Praise me! I want to be the most important! Why do you care so much about so many things?

But now, so many years later, I say: Thank you, Mother, for being what you were, for trying to develop me in every way.

Kisvárda was just a little town. It's where I began, where I yearned to be away from. I didn't think I could take a large enough breath there. Yet the memories of my teens are crowded not only with teen pains but also with precious hours spent with dear friends in a house so alive with interests, thoughts, activities, conversations, dancing, playing, and falling in and out of love that my house —the whole town—seemed to be bursting apart.

But there were other things, too—bad things. I cannot count the times I was called a "dirty Jew" while strolling down Main Street, Hungary. Sneaky whispers: "Dirty Jew." No, "Smelly Jew"—that's what I heard even more often. Anti-Semitism, ever since I can remember, was the crude reality. It was always present in the fabric of life. It was probably so everywhere, we thought, but surely so in Hungary—most certainly in Kisvárda.

They really hate us, I would think. It certainly felt that way. You couldn't hide from it. You couldn't run from it. It was everywhere. It was thinly veiled, when it was veiled at all. It was just under the skin. It was hard to live with. But we did. We knew no other way.

Each "Heil Hitler!" speech on the radio made things worse. And such speeches were on the radio constantly. Not many people understood German in my part of Hungary, but the radio was blasting away Hitler's speeches, and the frenzy of the incessant "Heil Hitlers!" made the Hungarian gentiles feel a camaraderie, a one-ness, with the mad orator. It also made us Jews cringe in the very depths of our souls. It made us fear the people with whom we had shared this town for generations.

What could we do?

Give us a patch of earth that is free of anti-Semitism!

We were afraid. Our neighbors, we knew, would be Hitler's willing accomplices when the bell would toll. And the bell tolled.

On Monday morning, May 29, 1944, the ghetto was evacuated. Jews, thousands upon thousands of Jews—every shape and form, every age, with every ailment, those whose Aryan blood was not Aryan enough, those who had changed their religion, oh, so long ago—dragged themselves down the main street toward the railroad station for what the Germans called "deportation." Upon their backs, bundles and backpacks—the compulsory "fifty kilos of your best clothing and food" (which the Germans could later confiscate in one simple operation).

And the Hungarian townspeople, the gentiles—they were there, too. They stood lining the streets, many of them smiling, some hiding their smiles. Not a tear. Not a good-bye. They were the good people, the happy people. They were the Aryans.

"We are rid of them, those smelly Jews," their faces read. "The town is ours!"

Main Street, Hungary.

A NEW MODE
OF TRAVEL

WE DRAG OURSELVES to the railroad station. The sun is mercilessly hot. People are fainting, babies screaming. We, the young and healthy teenagers, are totally spent. What must the old, the sick, feel? Totally stripped of our dignity, leaving the town we were born in, grew up in—what happens after this long wait? Where are we off to?

I am ready to go. Away from my cradle of love. Away from where every pebble and every face are familiar. Those familiar faces now reflect gladness. I must be away before I learn to hate them. I shall not return.

You, my former neighbors, I cannot live with you again. You could have thrown a morsel of sadness our way while we were dragging ourselves down Main Street. But you didn't. Why?

Please take me away from here. I don't know these people. I don't ever want to know them. I cannot detect the difference between them and the SS, so I'll go with the SS.

Soon we are packed into the cattle cars . . . cars with barred windows, with planks of wood on the bars, so that no air can enter or escape . . . seventy-five to a car . . . no toilets . . . no doctors . . . no medication.

I am menstruating. There is no way for me to change

my napkin . . . no room to sit . . . no room to stand
. . . no air to breathe. This is no way to die. It offends
even death. Yet people are dying all around me.

We squeeze my mother into a sitting position on the
backpack. Her face has an otherworldly look. She knows
she will not live. But she wants us to live, desperately. All
these years I've carried with me her face of resignation
and hope and love:

> Stay alive, my darlings—all six of you. Out there, when
> it's all over, a world is waiting for you to give it all I gave
> you. Despite what you see here—and you are all young
> and impressionable—believe me, there is humanity out
> there, there is dignity. I will not share it with you, but it's
> there. And when this is over, you must add to it, because
> sometimes it is a little short, a little skimpy. With your
> lives, you can create other lives and nourish them. You
> can nourish your children's souls and minds, and teach
> them that man is capable of infinite glory. You must be-
> lieve me. I cannot leave you with what you see here. I
> must leave you with what I see. My body is nearly dead,
> but my vision is throbbing with life—even here. I want
> you to live for the very life that is yours. And wherever I'll
> be, in some mysterious way, my love will overcome my
> death and will keep you alive. I love you.

And that frail woman of love lived until Wednesday.

THE ARRIVAL

WE HAVE ARRIVED. We have arrived where? Where are we?

Young men in striped prison suits are rushing about, emptying the cattle cars. "Out! Out! Everybody out! Fast! Fast!"

The Germans were always in such a hurry. Death was always urgent with them—Jewish death. The earth had to be cleansed of Jews. We already knew that. We just didn't know that sharing the planet for another minute was more than this superrace could live with. The air for them was befouled by Jewish breath, and they must have fresh air.

The men in the prison suits were part of the Sonderkommandos, *the people whose assignment was death, who filled the ovens with the bodies of human beings, Jews who were stripped naked, given soap, and led into the showers, showers of death, the gas chambers.*

We are being rushed out of the cattle cars. Chicha and I are desperately searching for our cigarettes. We cannot find them.

"What are you looking for, pretty girls? Cigarettes?

You won't need them. Tomorrow you will be sorry you were ever born."

What did he mean by that? Could there be something worse than the cattle-car ride? There cannot be. No one can devise something even more foul. They're just scaring us. But we cannot have our cigarettes, and we have wasted precious moments. We have to push and run to catch up with the rest of the family. We have just spotted the back of my mother's head when Mengele, the notorious Dr. Josef Mengele, points to my sister and me and says, *"Die zwei."* This trim, very good-looking German, with a flick of his thumb and a whistle, is selecting who is to live and who is to die.

Suddenly we are standing on the "life" side. Mengele has selected us to live. *But I have to catch up with my mother.*

Where are they going?

Mama! Turn around. I must see you before you go to wherever you are going. Mama, turn around. You've got to. We have to say good-bye. Mama! If you don't turn around I'll run after you. But they won't let me. I must stay on the "life" side.

Mama!

MY POTYO,
MY SISTER

HOW COULD I have ever loved this much?

I had permission to bathe her. To diaper her. To burp her. To rock her. To love her.

She was "my" baby.

She would be an old woman now, and I still cannot deal with having lost her.

The day we arrived in Auschwitz, there were so many people to be burned that the four crematoriums couldn't handle the task. So the Germans built big open fires to throw the children in. Alive? I do not know. I saw the flames. I heard the shrieks.

Is that the way you died, Potyo? Is that the way?

ONLY A NUMBER

SIX MILLION is only a number.
But each was somebody's mother, somebody's child,
somebody's lover, somebody's bride.
Potyo was just thirteen; she was my sister.
She had the wisdom of a child of war.
She was full of fear, yet tiptoed with tenderness,
laughter, and love in a world of madmen.
She was a weeping willow, a song of sorrow,
a poem of infinite beauty.
"Why does Hitler hate me? Why does he love hate,
  Mama?
I am only thirteen; I have songs yet to learn,
games yet to play.
Give me time to live, give me time to die.
Mama, how can I do all the living in just an inch of
  time?"
On a wretched piece of earth,
an alien land of terror and chaos,
on another planet called Auschwitz,
Mengele points at Potyo—
Ring-around-a-rosy,
pocket full of posies,
ashes, ashes . . .

GRAVE

LIFE DENIED US the grace of a grave. Just a grave for my mother, my sister, my other sister. Just a grave to bring flowers to.

Is a Jew that low that a Jew cannot even have a grave? Even death is too good for a Jew?

I am not sentimental. I am not conventional. Yet I crave so a small piece of earth, a testimony that I too had a mother, that this planet is mine too, so the salt of my tears on that little mound might make me part of the whole scheme of things.

The smoke has vanished, and only I remember it. And nothing marks that noble mother but my heart.

You beast! Give me the body, that frail little body. I want to bury it.

"EAT SHIT"

IT IS JUST getting dark. We have been in Auschwitz for several hours. My mother has been dead for several hours. Little, dearest Potyo, too. It is Wednesday, May 31, 1944.

We are in this huge wet place. Thousands of us. They call it the showers. They call it disinfection, whatever that means. The SS are all around. Orders are being shrieked in a language we hardly understand, presumably German. The words sound like *"Louse! Louse! Louse!"* It seems to mean *"Rush! Rush! Rush!"*

We are being shoved, pushed, lined up. Some girls are working away in a fury. Only the work is unbelievable. We have never seen anything like it before. They are shaving the heads of the new arrivals. And their pubic hair. And their underarms. The furious speed is unbelievable. What they are doing is unbelievable. Within seconds, Chicha is somebody else. Some naked-headed monster is standing next to me. Some naked-headed monster is standing next to her.

That's all there is? The two of us? A few hours ago we were a large family. Where is everybody?

There is someone over there in that big crowd. She looks familiar. That shaved thing is someone Chicha and

I seem to know. And next to her there is another. She looks familiar too. They are staring at us as well. We must know them. But we can't recognize them because they look so awful.

We inch toward each other. Is that you? Is that you? It's Regina. It's Cipi. They are our sisters. There are four of us.

What happened? What happened, darlings? There are four of us. We are a big family. We just found two sisters. They just found us. My God, we are so happy!

What happened? That German who whistled while pointing some people to the left and some people to the right turned us all around in front of some horribly smoky place and made another selection. He took us out of the group, and they brought us here, and now there are four of us. We are so happy, and we look so terrible. What did they do to us, and where are we? What is going to happen?

Suddenly, in the midst of this chaos, this insanity, somebody steps through the window of our building and recognizes us, these four naked-headed monsters. He shakes our shoulders, tears rolling down his face. "Listen to me. Listen! Eat whatever they give you. Eat. If they give you shit, eat shit. Because we must survive. We have to pay them back!"

And within seconds, my brother disappears through the window.

PHILIP

PHILIP, the caring Philip, the involved Philip, who managed to become some sort of ghetto official in Kisvárda so that at certain hours he would be permitted to leave the ghetto on "official" business. I don't know exactly what he did, but I do know that on the outside he would try to negotiate help for those on the inside.

Philip was overworked, exhausted, and every move he made was truly in the service of others. He was that kind of child, that kind of teenager. He is that kind of man. It is natural for Philip to be responsible to others. It was that way for my mother. Philip, more than any of us, is like my mother, whose heart truly was governed by the words "I am my brother's keeper." There are people like that. To be rendered totally helpless is probably more painful for such a person than for the rest of us.

Auschwitz lent itself to nothing. What could one do there to be a socially conscious human being? What could one do there to be a human being at all? With all odds against him, Philip found a way. He devised a means of communication. He was in a men's *Lager* some distance away, separated from us, as each *Lager* was, by electrified barbed-wire fences. One touch meant electro-cution.

Somehow Philip acquired a knife. He found pieces of wood and began to carve messages: "My four sisters are in *Lager* C. Their name is Katz. Whoever finds this piece of wood, please keep tossing it over the fences until it reaches *Lager* C." And miraculously, the messages al-ways reached us. Daily, the "mailmen" of Auschwitz, an unbroken chain of sufferers, would deliver the wood communication. Daily, at approximately the same spot, at approximately the same time, we would be standing there waiting for our "mail" from our ingenious brother, from the keeper of our souls. And the communication would always bear the same message: "You must sur-vive. You must live. You simply must. We not only have to pay them back. That is not reason enough. We must build a future free of bloodshedding."

And though on planet Auschwitz one was reduced to being an animal, Philip, your wooden gifts might have contributed to our survival. They just might have. So thank you, Philip.

Three weeks of wood blessings gave us a feeling of very special comfort, and we began to rely on those in-animate rechargers of our weakening spirit. Then the messages stopped. We stood at the usual spot for endless hours, endless days and weeks. We refused to accept the real message. Philip is no longer with us. He has left us. His legacy is lodged somewhere in our tortured hearts, but his body is gone—up in smoke, or where?

In 1945, when we were already in America, the mail-man in New York bore a letter from an American soldier in Germany to my father. The soldier told us that he had liberated Philip but that Philip had a bullet wound in his leg. Philip was now in a hospital. He had survived six concentration camps, and he would be with us when he recovered.

Bless you, soldier.

Bless you, Philip, keeper of our souls, brother of man.

THE BABY

MOST OF US are born to live—to die, but to live first. You, dear darling, you are being born only to die. How good of you to come before roll call though, so your mother does not have to stand at attention while you are being born. Dropping out of the womb onto the ground with your mother's thighs shielding you like wings of angels is an infinitely nicer way to die than being fed into the gas chamber. But we are not having *Zählappell,* so we can stand around and listen to your mother's muffled cries.

And now that you are born, your mother begs to see you, to hold you. But we know that if we give you to her, there will be a struggle to take you away again, so we cannot let her see you because you don't belong to her. You belong to the gas chamber. Your mother has no rights. She only brought forth fodder for the gas chamber. She is not a mother. She is just a dirty Jew who has soiled the Aryan landscape with another dirty Jew. How dare she think of you in human terms?

And so, dear baby, you are on your way to heaven to meet a recent arrival who is blowing a loving kiss to you through the smoke, a dear friend, your maker—your father.

CASTING
IN AUSCHWITZ

IT IS A BEAUTIFUL sunny Sunday. Summertime in Auschwitz. The crematoriums are taking a well-deserved rest. An easing of tension is hovering in the air. The sun must be healing our souls, burning out the pain from deep inside. There is something just a little bit different. They are leaving us alone a bit. The constant regimenting seems somewhat eased. What is it? Why? For whatever reason, it feels so good.

The little redheaded *Kapo* is busily scurrying about, asking all kinds of questions—who can sing what, play what instrument, recite what poem—the instant casting director. There will be a concert this afternoon in the *Lagerstrasse* for all to enjoy—the most unlikely cultural event on the face of the earth.

Regina, known for her magnificent dramatic power in reciting poetry, is chosen. She can fuse heaven and hell when she recites the words "At the sight of this, even the mute will speak." And there is a cello, a violin, a flute. The musicians play sitting on chairs. (Chairs? We haven't seen one since we left home.) Thousands of people are sitting on the ground, in the sun, incredulously soaking in the sounds.

What does this all mean? Will there be a change? Have

the Germans suddenly realized that we too have souls to be fed? Will they also feed our bodies? What does this all mean? Is this true? Or are we insane? Have they really succeeded and are we seeing imaginary things, hearing imaginary sounds in our tortured heads, sounds we vaguely remember to have loved? Please, somebody, tell us what is happening.

And somebody—or, rather, something—does. Airplanes are flying over our heads. The Germans are taking pictures of the humane treatment we are receiving in the legendary Auschwitz. The world will soon have proof of Germany's humanity to Jews.

MUSELMANNS

SELECTIONS. Selections. Selections. To weed out the *Muselmanns.* To be a lone person in *Lager* C was perhaps a blessing. To have sisters still alive, not to be alone, was a blessing too, but fraught with tests daily, hourly: When this day ends, will there still be four of us?

If you are sisterless, you do not have the pressure, the absolute responsibility to end the day alive. How many times did that responsibility keep us alive? I cannot tell. I can only say that many times when I was caught in a selection, I knew I had to get back to my sisters, even when I was too tired to fight my way back, when going the way of the smoke would have been easier, when I wanted to, when it almost seemed desirable. But at those times, I knew also that my sisters, aware that I was caught up in a selection, not only wanted me to get back to them—they expected me to get back. The burden to live up to that expectation was mine, and it was awesome.

Does staying alive not only for yourself, but also because someone else expects you to, double the life force? Perhaps. Perhaps.

Regina, more vulnerable than the rest of us, pleaded with us, oh, so often, "If I'm separated from you, if they

should take me on transport, don't count on me. Alone,
I won't make it. I don't want to make it. Whatever effort
I am making now is all for you. I no longer care to live—
unless, and only if, we are together. The minute we're
separated, I'll be on my way to the crematorium, and
that will be fine with me. You are forcing me to stay
alive, and I'm so tired."

Regina hardly slept—much less so than the rest of us.
The terror of being separated kept her awake. Only the
terror of separation, not fear of death. We pleaded with
her incessantly to promise to fight for her life should we
be separated. She pleaded with us incessantly not to ask
this much.

The responsibility of staying alive had its own inherent
torture. At times it doubled the alertness, at times I
wished I were alone, not to be asked to go constantly, on
a twenty-four-hour basis, against the tide. After all, the
business of Auschwitz was death. It is not everywhere
that death is so easily to be gotten.

I am tired. Let me go. . . . No, we won't. Our business is life.

My darling sisters, you are asking too much. And I am
asking too much of you. Yet the insanity of Auschwitz
must be imbued with meaning if *living* is to be contin-
ued, and the only meaning to living has to be for the four
of us to be where the sun shines, or the smoke blackens
the sky. All of us. Together.

Chicha was working in the *Unterkunft.* Some of the
fifty kilos of belongings that we had lugged on our backs
the day they dragged us to the railroad station for deportation were sorted out in the *Unterkunft.* That is where
Chicha's tears poured on my brother's pajamas when she
recognized the patch my mother had sewn on them. The
Unterkunft was one of the few places where so-called

work was performed in *Lager* C. *Lager* C was a *Vernichtungslager*, an annihilation *Lager*. The Germans kept us there not for work but to become *Muselmanns,* crematorium fodder.

Have you ever seen a *Muselmann?* Have you ever weighed 120 pounds and gone down to 40? Something like that—not quite alive, yet not quite dead. Can anyone, can even I, now picture it?

The *Unterkunft* was a place where on a few occasions you could go undetected while stealing something—the word for it was "organizing"—and the occasions when one could organize were very, very few. But Chicha once brought out a knife hidden in her shoes, and when we sliced our bread (Was it really bread? It tasted like sawdust.) into paper-thin miracles, we were able to delude ourselves that we had a lot of food, that our daily ration was really bigger than we thought.

Of course, the delusion lasted only a little while. The incredible hunger quickly reminded us of the lie. But lie we did. In our minds it was one more act of defiance: *"You see, Hitler, we are smarter than you. This will keep* Muselmann*ship away from us."*

Hell, no, it didn't. Our eyes sank deeper. Our skin rotted. Our bones screamed out of our bodies. Indeed, there was barely a body to house the mind, yet the mind was still working, sending out the messages *"Live! Live!"*

On this day the SS invaded Block 10 through both the front and the back entrances of the barracks. At other times, they would surprise us by coming in through only one entrance. That left a possibility of slipping out the other, escaping the selection—a slim possibility, but still some were able to slip out to the *Lagerstrasse* and be relatively safe until the next selection. After all, an hour of life is an hour of life. Why not make a run for it? It became a way of life, a way of death postponement.

Not this day. On this day Mengele came with his air of superiority to exercise his superior judgment with his right thumb and his left thumb: *This is a* Muselmann. *This is not—not yet.* He did this with an air of elegance. Cool and elegant. Yes, that was Mengele.

Caught in the trap, we were all hysterical—one thousand prisoners locked without hope in Block 10. The whole SS operation had taken but a few minutes.

Suddenly, with an awesome life instinct, Cipi, Regina, and I began to mimic the *Stubendiensts,* the Jewish *Kapos,* in their screaming, so as to appear to belong to them and thus escape the selection. Chicha, working in the *Unterkunft,* by now must know that Mengele is in Block 10. We must get out of here, we thought, back to her. Also, once again, we must survive. And so we screamed with an air of importance, as if we had assigned duties, as if we belonged to the wretched leadership. We screamed incoherently. We looked important. "Move! Don't move! This way! That way!" Anything, so long as we could convince the SS that we were working in Block 10, that we were aiding the beast. Our struggle for survival was now keener than at any other time. The seconds that separated us from death overwhelmed us with a reality we had never felt with any other selection. Both doors were bolted. Escape was impossible. But we could not be selected to die. We had to remain in Block 10 with those chosen to live. In the past, after the selection, the *Muselmanns* had always been led away to the ovens. That was the way it was always done. That's why we had to stay behind.

But now came the Nazis' evil ingenuity. This time, they reversed their procedure. This time, they led a group of prisoners out as usual, but now, after our insane struggle to remain behind, as we looked around, we found ourselves surrounded not by the so-called healthy ones, but by the *Muselmanns,* the crematorium fodder.

No! No! No! We won't go to the crematorium. Not yet. Not now. With nothing to lose but our lives, Cipi, Regina, and I rushed to one of the two bolted doors now being guarded by an emaciated inmate. With a power that emanates not from the body but from the spirit, we charged forward. The skeletal guard stepped out of our way, and we crashed against the door. The bolt snapped. The door gave way. And we were outside in the *Lagerstrasse.*

And there—fully expecting us, I am sure—was Chicha. "Chicha, Chicha! Don't cry!"

IRMA GRESE AND CHICHA

IS THE FACE a mirror? Is that mirror incapable of recording so much cruelty that it makes a complete turnabout and records beauty instead? How else could Irma Grese have been so perfectly beautiful? Flawless skin. A head of naturally blond hair. Almost perfect features. Who made this beautiful beast? Who was responsible for this mockery?

Irma Grese—dressed in immaculate SS uniform, usually with a light-blue shirt, a silver pistol in her holster, a huge dog at her side. The beautiful monster, our *Oberscharführerin,* our twice daily visitor, trailing her merciless terror behind her. Bisexual.

It is said that Chicha appeals to her. This manifests itself only in the fact that she always recognizes her and either tortures her more than the others or (on one occasion) does not send her off to die. This was the extent of her lesbian behavior toward Chicha. But torture her she did, in a fiendish manner, one particular afternoon.

Lager C, our *Lager,* was designed to hold 32,000 prisoners, 1,000 in each *Block* (barracks). On this late summer afternoon, the 32,000 prisoners, in rows of five, were once again being counted—*Zählappell,* they called it—and Grese was doing the counting. This was often a sham, with the SS claiming that a prisoner was missing, and therefore we would have to stand upright in line until every single prisoner was accounted for. Indeed, the SS needed no excuses, and certainly no one had ever escaped, but the device must have amused them, so frequently did they resort to it.

Now, as Grese counted, she came not from the *Lagerstrasse*—where we could see her approaching and thus ready ourselves to stand up straight—but instead from behind the *Blocks*. Such surprises always worked in favor of the SS and left us more helpless than before. At the rear of a column of *Fünferreihe* (rows of five prisoners), a girl was sitting on the ground to gather enough strength to stand erect for the moment when Grese would appear.

At *Zählappell* all prisoners must stand erect for whatever number of hours the roll call lasts. It is one of the sacred rituals. Any deviation is a mortal sin. In retrospect, it seems to me that not standing erect was a subtle sign of the spirit ebbing away, the readiness to be off to the *Kremchy* (the crematorium). This is, perhaps, too broad a generalization; nonetheless, the conclusion is inescapable, because the life force seems to have pushed us always to stand straight for just one more *Zählappell*. I did not think of it then, but what, if not the life force, made me stand erect with a 104-degree fever, with typhus so severe that our dear emaciated doctor friend, a fellow prisoner, kept saying, "At home, with the best of care, you would have died long ago"?

The girl resting on the ground was caught in the act by Grese. But Grese attributed the "crime" not to the girl, but to Chicha. Grese's attraction to Chicha, as her whole life did, took an aberrant form. She yanked Chicha out of the line to punish her. She dragged her to the center of the *Lagerstrasse* for all to see how crime does not pay. She made her kneel, lifted Chicha's arms high in the air, and placed two heavy rocks in her hands. She then ordered Chicha to hold her arms straight up for the duration of the *Zählappell.* *"And no wavering of the arms! If you do, you'll die! I'll return to check on you."* And so she did, over and over again, taunting Chicha, *"Have you had enough? Do you like it?"* She would touch Chicha's arms with her whip. *"They are not straight enough. There you go."*

Thousands of eyes stared at the bonelike creature in the *Lagerstrasse* seemingly holding two mountains, so frail did she look in comparison to the rocks. She, the rock herself—with all the prisoners' eyes turned heavenward in prayer: "God, do not let her drop the rocks, because then she'll die, and a little bit of our spirit, our determination to live and tell this tale, will die with her. God, help us to imbue her with our unified spirit, keep her arms straight, keep our souls riveted to hers, and maybe we'll all live. Do not desert us now. The hour that pits good against evil is right here, right now, on this ugly piece of land, mutilated by gas chambers and crematoriums that devour by the millions the highest form of life, each of which took nine months to cry out. They cry no more. Their silence deafens Chicha's ears. Their silence straightens Chicha's arms. The chorus of the dead silently whisper in her soul, 'Keep your arms straight. Keep your arms straight. For the dead and for the living. For the dead and for the living.' "

A fury of thoughts rushed through our heads: *That human being out there on display in the* Lagerstrasse *is our sister. A halo is glowing around her shriveled body. Her strength is being tested ferociously. Her three sisters' strength is being tested ferociously, too. Will she make it? How much longer can we endure her endurance? Trust me! Trust us!*

The gentile woman from Budapest, she of noble birth, who was sent to Auschwitz because she had committed an unpardonable crime—she had helped her Jewish friends—I no longer remember her name, only her aristocratic face, drawn and hungry. She had been the fifth person in our *Fünferreihe*. She died in the ovens later, but now she was with us, and we loved her, and she loved us. There had not been any need for intellectual utterances for a long while now. Only the language of survival was of import here. Yet with her, on occasion, we actually talked of books. Strange must be the ways of the hungry, for even while the body is starving, the mind may crave nourishment too.

This gentile woman stood with us now as we watched Chicha, and her words will linger in my mind for all my days to come:

I had to save my friends. I just had to. Yet, through these months of suffering, I have thought of the luxurious ways of the privileged that I gave up. Yes, at times—ashamed as I am to say it—doubts, even regret, kept creeping into my head. But today [and she took a long, compassionate look at Chicha] I know with absolute certainty why I am here. This is where I belong. I could not be anywhere else. Guilt from a lavish life would tear my guts asunder while all of this is taking place around me. At this moment in history I belong here, with you, with the innocent, with Chicha, with her arms raised toward the heavens. I belong standing next to the three of you, caressing your wounded hearts, and I tell you with absolute certainty that she will make it.

As we stood there in our columns, endless hours passed. At last, Grese returned. She strode up to Chicha. She knew she had been defeated. "Put those rocks down," she said.

REGINA

IT IS NOW November 1944, six months after we arrived, and the four of us are still alive. We have avoided every single selection so far. But now it is Sunday morning, and there is a sudden selection—sudden, as always.

Regina, our little sister, is too young, too broken in spirit and body. She will not possibly be able to make it. She is all too ready for the oven. But it cannot happen. We must keep her alive. We love her too dearly.

Mengele is selecting a little distance away from us. He is selecting the *Muselmanns*, those who are totally emaciated, those who have no possibility of being chosen for work transport. He is selecting for the oven.

Suddenly, frantically, we try to make Regina healthier looking, older looking (she is only fifteen and a half). Mengele must not have his way. We will keep her alive.

One of us has a piece of cloth. We place it on Regina's head as a kerchief. We make her stand on tiptoes while she pleads that she has no strength for such superhuman efforts. We pinch her face to an unnatural redness . . .

Mengele passes her by.

This day the crematorium has been cheated of our precious sister. This day Hitler has lost and we have won—wit against might. We will live on for another day.

SERENITY

YES, SIX MONTHS in Auschwitz. And the four of us are still alive. And we are together—the single most important thing. We touch each other. Cipi, Chicha, Regina, Isabella—the four sisters together, and we seem to be alive. Dazed, weighing probably no more than forty, fifty, sixty pounds each, but words come out of our lips, so we must be alive. In sort of an otherworldly way.

We don't look like anything we have ever seen, but on the other hand, we no longer know what anything looks like. Or anyone. We live among *Muselmanns*. The whole world must be populated with *Muselmanns*. The Germans look like things we have seen before. They have ruddy cheeks, immaculate uniforms, but the sickness of their souls and the stench of death about them are so pervasive that we are not sure they are real.

We are pure and beautiful. We have nothing in common with them. They are Germans. We were born of mothers the smell of whose burning flesh permeates the air, but what were they born of? Who sired them?

The little baby born yesterday, whose mother remained alive because her pregnancy was not noticed, is off now to the crematorium. She was born only to die immediately. What was your hurry, little baby? Couldn't you have waited until the house painter was dead, so you could have lived? Couldn't the gods have arranged for a longer pregnancy so that evil, not life, would be murdered? For a moment, for just a moment, we had a real smell of a real life, and we touched the dear little one before she was wrapped in a piece of paper and quickly handed to the *Blockälteste* so the SS wouldn't discover who the mother was, because then she, too, would have had to accompany the baby to the ovens. That touch was so delicious. Are we ever to know what life-giving feels like? Not here. Perhaps out there, where they have diapers, and formulas, and baby carriages—and life.

And now it was November 1944. The business of Auschwitz had to be terminated because soon the Russians would march in, and the Germans were thinking: *Let's ship some of these* Muselmanns *on work transport and send the rest to the crematorium. Let's wrap up this whole Auschwitz business.*

Not many were left in *Lager* C, my *Lebensraum* for the past six months. They rounded us up. To go where? To the work transport? To the ovens? Which would it be? Does it matter? The four of us are together—that is what matters.

And they led us away from this heaven. I say "heaven" because, so far, each change we have gone through was for the worse. Perhaps the next one would make us long for what we have now. And yes, they took us to the crematorium.

We stood there all night, the smoke spewing out of the stacks furiously, bringing with it an illusion of warmth in the dread, cold November night. And the serenity we felt we will never forget. We had made it all the way here together. We cheated them out of the joy of tearing us in

four different directions. For a lone person, it didn't matter which way you went—you left no one behind. When
it was possible to save four members of the same family,
the only thing that mattered was that you all went the
same way. We are doing that now. This is the last stop.
Nothing can change this. We are leaving no one behind.
It is unalterable, but we feel a serenity that we never felt
before. We are together and can face whatever follows
the end of this long, silent, serene vigil. Together to the
ovens. A note of thanks, bitchy Fate.

But then the end of this chilly November night came.
And as had happened so many times before, the German
orders were changed. This crematorium-bound group
was ordered into an icy set of trains to be sent to another
concentration camp.

'Bye, Auschwitz. I will never see you again. I will always see you.

BIRNBAUMEL

AUSCHWITZ was behind us. Birnbaumel in eastern Germany was our new concentration camp home. It had a great advantage: It had no crematorium. It had a great disadvantage: It had no electrified fences that one could —as so many had done in Auschwitz—touch and die. The camp was at one end of the forest. The tank traps we dug were at the other end. To go from one to the other we had to march through the town, twice a day, coming and going. In the morning we were marched through the town, every day—a thousand wretched young women. The pity of that sight could make a beast weep. But not the Germans.

Church bells ringing. The smell of fresh bread from bakeries. Children going to school. The life of a small town. It was even a little bit like home. Then, toward evening, we were marched through the town again. But the Germans never saw us. Ask them. They never saw us. Come to think of it, they really didn't. It was beneath their Aryan dignity. We were just a lot of filthy Jews. Why even glance at us? In the comfort of their homes they probably cast gentle, loving gazes at their cats, or dogs, or whatever. They were sensitive. They were cultured. Germany was one giant concentration camp, with

Jews marching the length and breadth of the country, but these refined, sensitive Germans never saw us. Find me a German who ever saw me. Find me one who ever harmed us.

It was December, and there was this fat *Oberscharführer,* whose flesh alone would have kept him warm. He was one of our guards, and he used to stand by the fire we built in the forest, warming his huge rump, while chasing us away from the fire with the butt of his rifle. The fire, indeed, was necessary. We couldn't dig the earth. It was frozen. It had to be heated up first. Keep the earth warm. Not the Jews.

In that forest the fire of resistance kept my frozen body alive. My mother had told me not to aid my enemy. In that forest in Birnbaumel in December, I remembered her. I honored her and tried to keep myself alive.

I was a one-woman sabotage team. As soon as the Germans walked away, I would put down my shovel and stop digging. Digging to me symbolized digging my own grave. In reality, that was what it was. And even in that place, emaciated as my body was, it still housed a soul to be tended and cared for, and when I could nourish it, I did.

HITTING
THE ZELT

BIRNBAUMEL could hardly inspire anything, yet for some reason, I noticed my own fractured humanness there. The first night we arrived in Birnbaumel, I overheard some of the *Oberscharführer*'s instructions to his fellow SS. They were to choose ten *Kapos* from among the prisoners—one for every one hundred inmates. This was unlike Auschwitz, where there was one *Kapo* for every one thousand—not to mention the various ugly positions below the *Kapo*.

The German genius had, of course, variations of evil, one of which was to appoint torturers from among the inmates themselves. Brother against brother. Sister against sister. And if you survived long enough, you realized that the minutest advantage might help you make it through. In many cases the Germans realized their intentions. They succeeded in brutalizing some of us. But only some. Only some. A small number of people survived as much as five or six years. Dehumanization of such long duration can take a toll beyond all comprehension. I don't mean dehumanization only of the soul, but the simultaneous dehumanization of the body as well. The German hate bombardment, the teaching of hatred to their own people, was directed only at their souls (if indeed there were souls there to begin with). The German bodies were well nurtured with the food Hitler stole from country after country. But we drank urine and ate sawdust. You can't do that for long and remain brave and human and upright.

So when the time came, I was there to be chosen to be a *Kapo*. If I learn how to be a *Kapo*, I reasoned, who knows, we might stay alive and be there to greet our liberators. I owe it to my sisters to try to keep all of us alive. Ah, dear God, teach me how to be a *Kapo!*

And I was chosen. I was a *Kapo*. And using my new authority, I was able to assign Regina to be the toilet cleaner of the camp, Chicha to be the cleaner of our *Zelt* (an umbrellalike wooden barracks), and Cipi to be her assistant. All of this meant that they did not have to go out daily to dig in the forest and return with their legs frozen, as so many did.

One of my duties as *Kapo* was to round up those prisoners who tried to avoid going to the forest. This happened daily, and the SS woman in charge gave me a huge stick and showed me how to beat the runaways. Waving the stick in the air, I ran around the camp screaming orders as loud as I could. I tried to sound as brutal as possible, and I used the stick with as much might as I could muster. But at last I was caught by the SS. I was striking the walls of the *Zelt*, not the inmates. I simply couldn't. I didn't know how to lash out at someone who was as miserable as I was. I fell from grace with a thud. I had been a *Kapo* for two days. I wasn't shot, but from then on I was always recognized as the ex-*Kapo* who could never escape the trip to the forest.

MY HEART
IS BEATING

MY HEART is beating. Faster and faster. It will be me.
The *Oberscharführer* will choose me. I know he will.
Along with several others. To carry the dead girl to her
grave. I can dig the grave, but please, please don't choose
me to carry the body. Have mercy. I cannot carry the
dead body. Inside, deep in my being, I am just a child.
The dead, cold body I cannot touch. It makes me shiver.
Please. Please.

There is no crematorium in which to burn the dead in
Birnbaumel. The dead actually have to be buried, out
some distance from the camp. It is done at night, in the
ominous night, and I am frightened. So terribly frightened. Don't choose me.

But he does. And then the pitiful little band is off to
the hill to perform the sacred mission. Chicha is chosen
as a grave digger, and four others are chosen to carry the
body. We are off to a patch of earth in a foreign land
that is soaked with the blood of the innocent, the young,
the unfulfilled, the martyred children of martyred Jewish
mothers who dared to give life in an age of death.

I am about to slip my trembling palms under the
corpse when Chicha softly, compassionately, whispers in
my ear: "I will put my hands under the body, and you

put your hands on mine." Tears are rolling down my cheeks. Not for the dead girl, but for the goodness that is still alive, that refuses to be buried, however hard the madman tries to still the voice of God in man.

Rest in peace, young girl. The flickering stars above must be the weeping children of your womb. The womb, the glorious womb, the house that celebrates life, where life is alive, where the bodies of young girls are not carried out into the night. Rest in peace, young girl.

THE DAILY TRIP to the forest took its toll. Both my spirit and my body were decimated. Ill with typhus, I was finally put in the *Revier,* the concentration camp's version of a hospital, which resembled no hospital anyone has ever seen. You slept on the cold earth, you defecated right there, because you were no longer human enough to go out—and, of course, you were beaten for it.

The only advantage of being in the *Revier* was that you did not have to go out to the forest. You were lying mostly with people who could no longer walk, who were hopelessly ill with gangrene. The odor could drive you mad, but you no longer cared, because there were only a few more days of life left in you, and death would be welcome.

My sisters came every night to pump spirit into my near-death body. "Please, please make yourself live. We held on this long—it really would be sacrilegious to give up now. You must hold out. The Nazis' end must be near." And "Here is a tiny piece of bread," said Chicha. "You mustn't think that I took it away from myself. I really, really am not hungry."

And they came every night to pump life into me. I am

sure that I did not want to live. But every night, they were there, terror-stricken that the bone they called a sister was no longer alive.

But the bone had a heart that refused to stop beating. And the bone would greet the three sunken-eyed visitors.

JANUARY 22, 1945

WE ARE NOW in another German town. I think we are not far from Breslau. I think the town is Prauschnitz. That is how I remember it. It is Monday, January 22, 1945. It is the end of the workday. The town is rushing home. This time we are not marching through the center but are sort of mingling with the home-going towns-people. This time we aren't so painfully lined up by the SS guards, so terribly organized. This is very unlike the Germans. The system, it seems, is beginning to fall apart.

I have a curious, unreal feeling, one of almost being part of the grayish dusk of the town. But again, of course, you will not find a single German who lived in Prauschnitz who ever saw a single one of us. Still, we were there, hungry, in rags, our eyes screaming for food. And no one heard us. We ate the smell of smoked meats reaching our nostrils, blowing our way from the various shops. Please, our eyes screamed, give us the bone your dog has finished gnawing. Help us live. You wear coats and gloves just like human beings do. Aren't you human beings? What is underneath the coats?

Suddenly, in the open sewer to my side, there is a funny-looking inmate scurrying for a hiding place. May God be with you. Escape is impossible, but may you be the one who succeeds. For the guts you have, you deserve it.

And yes, she succeeded. She was out of sight, undetected. But a moment later she was back. She had crawled back to the line of prisoners.

"I couldn't leave you. I can't live while you die. We must all escape or perish together." That scrawny, scurrying thing was my sister.

Dear Chicha, how much longer will our pact hold? Must we all die unless we all survive together? We must learn to break the bond. Therein lies life. Our pact must end, else none will be left. We must soon be liberated, or we will soon die, because there is only a little bit of life left in us. We must make a new pact—each for herself. We can no longer fight for each other as before. There simply isn't enough life left in us. We must seek whatever there can be for us, any change at all, alone if it has to be. Let us learn a new way of life, of death. Please, let each of us understand this. The old pact must go. A new one must take its place. Somebody will have to live. Somebody must. No argument about this. It is final. We cannot all die. Somebody will have to keep this sturdy gene alive. Somebody must live to tell the tale.

THE BARN

THAT NIGHT we are at our new camp, which had been evacuated the night before by the thousands who had come before us. But there isn't enough room, and some of us are shoved into a barn. So here we are, the four of us, together with some other miserable creatures. As dawn approaches we try to bury ourselves deep in the hay. Perhaps the SS will not find us when he pokes around with his pitchfork for those who stubbornly insist on surviving.

When we left the forest camp in Birnbaumel the day before to walk in the freezing snow toward Bergen-Belsen, we didn't realize that we were being rushed so desperately because the Russian army was close behind us. Indeed, the Russians were so close that had we hidden ourselves somewhere in Birnbaumel, the Germans would not have had the time to look for us and we would have been liberated by the Russian army that very afternoon. But we didn't know that then. All we knew was that the Germans were in a hurry to take us farther west, and, if possible, we must not go. So now, in the barn, we dug ourselves deep into the hay.

When the Germans were ready to move on, they had no time to go looking separately for each prisoner who tried to escape. But they were not about to let their Jews go easily. They were too diabolical. So they began to cook potatoes. Soon the smell of food began to fill the air, and a moment later, the stubborn will to live that we had nourished for so long evaporated completely.

One by one we emerged from the haystack and staggered toward the food line. The smell of potatoes evidently was more powerful than the will to live. But by the time we reached the kettle, not a morsel was left.

Yes, the Germans were smarter than we—or, simply, not as hungry. Under those conditions, it was easy to play maddening games of death. The year 1945 was not the kind in which somebody could be smart. That time, that month, that day shames my soul now, because I am no longer hungry and I can't imagine how I could have sold my freedom for the smell of a potato.

The hay was all over. It was in our eyes, in our hair—it must have been mixed up with our brains. Yes, that's what it was, hay in the brains. How could we have imagined that we ever again would walk, talk, feel like human beings? We had tried to interfere with the work of the manufacturers of death, and you cannot do that. The Germans' bible was death, and humiliation, and dehumanization, and they succeeded so well that they destroyed our ability to reason, and we voluntarily leaped back into their arms. And so many decades later, it still hurts that the animals in those spick-and-span uniforms, in those shiny boots, had the cunning to lure us back to destruction by rubbing our noses in an aroma.

I curse you, even from the distance of these many years, for keeping me so hungry that it affected my brain and subordinated me to your evil. And my apologies to the animals for comparing you to them, because surely animals are more humane.

BACK IN THE LINE, the pitiful thousand, minus the few who did escape, the many who died, we are on our way to walk the infinite distance to Bergen-Belsen. Our pact now is not spoken but fully understood. Any of the four sisters is now allowed (meant in a deep emotional sense) to vanish, to die, to give up, to live. The faintest possibility of aiding each other morally or physically no longer exists.

Eastern Germany is bitter cold in January. There is a blizzard. Regina is coughing very badly. On one foot she has a torn leather shoe, on the other a Dutch wooden shoe. In the blizzard and with the uneven shoes, she can barely drag herself along. Between the four of us, we are missing one shoe, and whichever one tries to aid Regina by giving up a shoe will be the one to die. In the past, we always found a solution—an abnormal solution in an abnormal setting, but still, some kind of solution. But we cannot crack this one. For one of us, death is hours away. What to do? Is the life force strong enough yet to make us act if there is another opportunity? Will instinct guide us to survival? We don't know.

We are marching in the blizzard in *Fünferreihe*. Always five in a row. For the four of us, this was a special problem, because to be five in a row was the prisoners' responsibility. And so we always had to find an unattached girl for our row. And when we found one, it was never permanent, for sooner or later she died, was taken on transport or to the crematorium, or attached herself to someone else. It was a continuous struggle.

But now we are marching in the blizzard on a silent, deserted road. SS guards are in front, leading the column, on both sides, and in the rear. We have just reached a tiny village called Jagadschutz. Suddenly, Chicha notices a little house to her right. It is covered with snow, and no smoke is coming from the chimney. Chicha is on the outside of the column. Regina is next to her. I am next to Regina, and Cipi is next to me. The side guards have gone to the rear because some prisoners have escaped. Only the guards in the front remain, and they can't see us from their position.

In a flash, Chicha is running toward the house. Then Regina. Then I. There is no thinking on our parts. Not a word among us. Just one sister following the other.

Regina and I run to a tiny doghouse behind the main house and crawl inside. Everything is totally silent, deserted. Deep snow blankets the area. The scene is reminiscent of Christmas—"Peace on earth, good will toward men."

Crouched in the doghouse, we are not breathing. There is nothing but silence and terror. When will they kill us? Where are they? Why did we escape?

Slowly, carefully, we inch our way out. We crouch behind the doghouse. Silence again. Where is Chicha? Where is Cipi? Silence. Only silence.

Suddenly there is the sound of crackling snow on the

road. The *Oberscharführer,* with his dog, is coming back
from the slaughter—we heard the shots. He is cursing
the filthy Jews for slowing down the column by attempt-
ing to escape. He is utterly furious, mumbling to himself,
in a hurry to catch up with the group. We can see him
from our crouching position. He cannot see us.

But the dog will smell us. Regina and I automatically
grab our chests. What will it feel like—the bullet? Oh!
Oh! Please, please don't do it. Will it be in the chest or in
the head? Will it hurt terribly? Will we die immediately?
If not, will he shoot again?

Till now we have seen only other people die, and it
was awful. But this will be us. It will be me. Now we
know we are only seconds away from death, and it is
terrible. It would have been better if we hadn't seen him,
if our backs were to him. Then we wouldn't have known
in advance that we are going to be murdered. Cruel, ugly
Fate. At least not to know, not to see him point the rifle
at us.

God! God, help us! This once. You have not shown
us any mercy all these months. Have mercy. My chest
feels awful. Something will rip it apart in a second.
Can't you do something, God? Don't let us die. Not
this way. Not here. Not now. Not ever. Death, go
away—go! Please!

I have lived barely two decades. Regina is only sixteen.
Will nobody help us? Will this dog and this dog of a man
just rip us apart in a second? Somebody, please help us!
Isn't there anybody in this whole world who cares? We
haven't done anything. We have hardly lived. We have
known barely anything but war.

Where is my mother? She will protect us. Mama!
Where are you? Somebody is trying to kill your children.

The *Oberscharführer* is coming to kill us. He is coming closer . . . closer. He is right here.

He is gone.

What happened? Was the wind blowing our scent away from the dog? We are not dead. There is no bullet in our chests. . . . We are alive. . . . He is gone.

THE HOUSE

"ISABELLA, Regina, Cipi. Are you all here? Where are you? I am in the attic. I found a frozen cabbage, and it's delicious. Hurry, come up here; the house is empty; there's no one around. Are you all here?"

"No, Chicha, just the two of us—Regina and Isabella. Cipi probably ran into the next house, or the one after that. She's here somewhere, and when it's all safe, we'll find her."

"Then come on up and let's eat, before the Germans come back to kill us. Let's eat."

We run up to the attic. To Chicha. To the cabbage. To happiness.

Now, there is an ever so faint noise. We peer through a hole. The door downstairs is being opened with the very greatest caution. A terrified head can be seen looking around. Then another, and then a third.

With the voices of those whose death sentence has just been deferred, we cry out: "It is us! It is us!"

We run downstairs, quite certain by now that the house is deserted, and hug the three new arrivals, the three brave inmates who have also escaped. Cipi is not among them, but we are not worried. We are quite sure she is somewhere in the vicinity.

The people who had been living in the house must have been in an awful hurry to get away, for their milk had been left unrefrigerated and untouched. They had run in haste with their beloved Nazis toward western Germany. This little house is now ours, to do with as we like.

And what do we like?

Food! And we find it. In abundance. A pantry filled with smoked meat. An entire pig. Greasy, smoked, awful, marvelous, fantastic, glorious—all ours, to be eaten instantly, all of it, this very second. And we do.

We eat and eat—not eat, devour. Without a stop. Now the Nazis can do as they like. We have eaten. We are eating. And will eat until the second our lives are snuffed out. The only reason to live is to eat.

Oh, my stomach. It hurts. It hurts deliciously. It's filled. It cannot hold any more food. But that will not stop any of us. Eat. Eat.

There is no toilet indoors. We'll use that huge bin. We are alternating—eating and using the bin. We are eating while using the bin. Life is glorious. We want to live forever. We want to eat forever.

JANUARY 24, 1945

CIPI, CIPI, where are you? You were marching next to me. You saw me run when I saw Regina run. Regina ran only because she saw Chicha run. I ran only because I saw Regina run. Regina and I were certainly not thinking. Chicha must have been. She was the one to notice that the SS men had gone to the rear. She was on the outside of the column. Her act, I feel, was more than just instinct. It was a sudden flash of evaluation, of assessing the situation. It was a moment that called for crystal-clear thinking. And she was capable of it. We merely followed.

Cipi, how could you not have followed? How could you not? Were you not the one who said that no matter in what shape—legless, armless—you want to survive, we all must survive? You said that over and over again. What became of your will to live? Were you afraid that we would be caught? Were you so paralyzed by fear that you could only march ahead with the devil? Did their intimidation eat into your soul that deeply? I cannot understand.

For all these many years I have tried to grapple with this awesome riddle, and I cannot come to terms with it. You were supposed to follow us blindly because our instincts were the direct opposite of theirs—therefore, what we did had to be right. They chewed up your soul. They chewed it up and I was left crying. Had I known, I would have pulled you along. Was I supposed to pull you? Was I supposed to tug at your ragged sleeve? Was I?

Then, much later, others who saw you, and lived to tell, spoke your words: "My sisters, they have escaped. They will live. May the gods be with them and help them every step of the way!"

They told us how, on your way to Bergen-Belsen, you made several attempts to escape, how your proud spirit reasserted itself. But it was too late, and you were caught.

They told us how you begged the murderers to kill you, but they wouldn't because they knew you had lost your sisters to freedom, and to be alone is more agonizing than a bullet.

They told us how your agony drew smiles to their foul lips, and how they dragged you for three long weeks on the death march to Bergen-Belsen.

And they told us that you still lived when the British liberated Bergen-Belsen. But then you lived no more.

Cipi!

JANUARY 24, 1945— EVENING

WE DARE NOT GO OUT during the day. It is evening now. There is a chicken in captivity in the yard. We must eat that too. Regina steps out to get the chicken. She doesn't know how to kill it, so she slams it against the wall and reappears with the prize.

Chicken soup—no matter where, no matter how—is a cure for everything. That is the old adage, and it works. Our spirits soar at the smell of it. My mother would be happy.

Suddenly, the lights go out. Chicha says the Germans must have evacuated the town. They have cut the power.

The dreamer dreams. The rest of us are skeptical, laughing at her dreams. We are feasting on the last supper.

REGINA, I SALUTE YOU

YOU WERE so vulnerable, so terrified of being separated. The terror kept you awake in Auschwitz more than the rest of us. You barely slept. Our hearts were weeping for you more than for any of us.

But, Regina, when we couldn't, you killed the chicken for us to eat. And though you were unable to kill the memory of the madman, you were alive and well when he killed himself. And if loyalty can be fierce, you are fierce. You killed the chicken, and you would have killed anything in sight for your sisters. You were the little mother to us, forever going to Prauschnitz to organize, to find food and clothing for us after we were liberated.

And later, you were the mother hen, cutting up a blanket to sew into a coat for me because I was cold. The endless care. The endless concern. Our complete confidence that we could rely on you. We always blessed you. Did you know that?

But above all, in spite of your premonitions, in spite of your fear of separation, in spite of your words "Do not count on me to stay alive," in spite of yourself—your life force, the landscape of your spirit, was greater than all of your words, and you remained alive.

Regina, I salute you.

JANUARY 25, 1945

AND WE EAT and eat and eat. There is an orgy of smoked pig, but not a crust of bread to go with it. All that grease and fat without bread is murder on our stomachs, but the cycle of eating and shitting does not stop. Is there food enough on this planet to satiate the remnants of Auschwitz? It does not seem so. Eat, shit, and back to bed under the warm down covers.

We are all in bed, resting between the heavy chores of eating, emptying our sickly stomachs, and waiting for liberation or death. Suddenly the door opens, and a short man with a huge mustache is standing there. He is wearing civilian clothes and is unarmed.

Is he the last man we will ever see? Who is he? "I advise you to leave," says the man. "The Germans are all around. They'll soon discover you and kill you. Leave."

"We have no place to go," we reply. "Where should we go? . . . Is there no chance to be liberated? . . . Is it this house you want? . . . The contents? . . . We don't want the house. . . . We just want to eat and rest. . . . Let us stay. . . . Don't frighten us anymore. . . . Leave us in peace, to live or to die."

The man, a Pole brought to Germany with so many others after the *Blitzkrieg,* vanishes and leaves behind a renewed feeling of terror. The time is about 11 A.M., Thursday. Back to the food. Back to bed. I am wearing a little blue cotton dress for a nightgown. I found it in one of the armoires. Some of the nightgowns worn by the others are fancy. They came from the carefully organized dowry chest left behind. Indeed, everything was left behind. Had we not been so busy eating, we could have had quite a fashion show of embroidered undies. But we had better things to do. We had to count the hours left to us.

Will the little man with the big mustache inform on us? Will he keep our existence secret? What will he do? If we start on the road, we'll surely be discovered. We must stay. It clearly is the only choice. Out there is certain death. In here, at least, there is food. Do we have any allegiance? Yes. To food. Back under the covers. Our depression is total. Our house is at the end of the road. And this, indeed, is the end of the road.

It is now 1 P.M. The deadly silence is broken sharply, suddenly. There are noises, harsh noises—of trucks, horses, tanks, war machinery of every kind. Did the whole German army come to get us? All this for six skeletons? An orgy of deadly machinery for a handful of bones?

You stupid, stupid Hitler. We haven't any guns. We couldn't possibly harm you. We don't know anything about the business of killing. You are the genius of death. We mean to give life, to cherish it, to cradle it. You, army, turn back. Your opponent doesn't know how to kill.

Carefully, terrified, the six of us tiptoe to the window. We move the curtain ever so slightly so that we may see the life-snuffers making their deadly moves toward us. And there is so much to be seen. Tanks, trucks, ammunition carriers, blood-splattered soldiers, bedraggled soldiers—worn, dying, on horses, on foot, pitiful, not brave, just spent, wretched looking. They have no nationality, no politics, no ideology. They are just battle weary and worn. Who are they? What do they want from us? Why don't they go home and get bandaged with gauze and love? Men, you need care. Do not spend the little strength you have on killing us. Seek solace, not hate. Seek out your children. They need your love. They need to give you theirs. Stop killing. Stop it.

But wait. Wait. These men are wearing strange uniforms. They are not German or Hungarian. They are unfamiliar. And there is a red flag—red, red.

What is red?

Red is not German, red is . . . Russian.

We are . . . we are—What? What are we? We are . . . we are . . . we are liberated!

Barefoot, wearing only a single garment each, we all surge out into the brutal January frost and snow of eastern Germany and run toward the troops. Shrieks of joy. Shrieks of pain. Shrieks of deliverance. All the pent-up hysteria accumulated over years of pain and terror suddenly released.

I have never since heard sounds like those we uttered, sounds released from the very depths of our being. The sheer force of it must have scattered the ashes of Auschwitz to every corner of the universe, for our cries of joy suddenly turned into a bitter wail: "We are liberated! We are liberated! But where are they all? They are all dead!"

BOOK TWO
LIBERATION

THE RUSSIANS

THE ADVANCING RUSSIANS have taken Jagadschutz, the village in which we have been hiding since our escape from the Nazi death march to Bergen-Belsen.

Our shaved heads tell them who we are. A Russian soldier rips the dog tag with my prison number, 79212, off my neck. "You don't need this anymore. You are free!" His words are in Russian, which I don't understand, but his meaning is clear.

The tough Red Army men are good-hearted and compassionate. They give us apples and bread, whatever food they have.

Some time later, however, when pounds have begun to stick to our bodies, some of the soldiers, drunk and lustful, begin to see us as women; and, virginal young girls that we are, we try to save ourselves by fleeing through house windows, hiding in closets, or crawling under beds.

I pull a sock, full of holes, over my hairless head, distort my face to give it an imbecilic look, and walk as though crippled. I am not ready to be raped, even by my saviors, and, somehow, each time I escape having to taste first love through foul breath in a desperate land of cruelty and war.

My sisters, Chicha and Regina, also manage to save themselves. By now we have discovered that there were thirty girls who escaped in our vicinity. But no one has seen Cipi.

Little Roszi, a Hungarian girl, was raped. She thinks she is pregnant. She walks with a crazed, dazed look on her face. We comfort her without really being able to help.

Three other escapees, our "partners," are Polish. They are able to communicate with the Russian officers and become their lovers. They seem to be knowing, experienced women. They tell me and my sisters that they are shielding us with their own bodies. They begin to order us about, making us clean the deserted house we have "appropriated." They make us cook while they wait for their warring heroes, who visit them whenever they can get back from the fierce battles raging around Breslau. Our Polish friends become our pseudoslavemasters.

The house is crowded with lovers. Chicha, Regina, and I still "live" here, but many a night we sleep in another deserted house across the road. A middle-aged woman, who survived with her daughter, is with us in the other house.

One night the woman places her daughter on a cot in the anteroom, covers her with layers of down-filled comforters, and lies down on top of her. It is one of those ugly times when drunken heroes seem to be everywhere. I am ill with fever, wearing nothing but a very short blue-and-white cotton something and lying in the same bed with my sister Regina. The dying flame of a tiny chunk of candle provides the sole illumination.

Two drunken soldiers suddenly charge into our room. They ignore the older woman and her hidden daughter in the anteroom and blow out the struggling, expiring candle. Barefoot, Regina and I run out of the house and across the snow-covered stretch that leads to our headquarters house, where the officers and the three Polish girls are making love to the sounds of cannon nearby. We know our friends will protect us.

The frustrated soldiers, our would-be lovers, follow us into the white-blanketed night and fire their guns in the air.

Inside our original home, one of the Russian officers speaks to us. He speaks Yiddish to me and, for special comfort, tucks me into bed between him and his Polish girlfriend. As I fall into a weary sleep I am aware of my bedmates changing places in order to love away the night.

THE FIGHTING near Breslau is fierce, but our area is clear of the enemy. The Russians in Jagadschutz are now trying to "govern." The fleeing Germans had abandoned their old, their sick, and their livestock. The Russians assign the liberated concentration camp women to cattle duty.

Every day we are forced to feed and clean the cows. The necessity is clear, but we are reluctant to care for the animals. Every morning the Russians have to root us out from our hiding places. We are not cooperative. We have to be forced to work with cud and dung. We know nothing of cattledom, are exhausted from prisondom. We are tired and spent. We want to be cared for ourselves, not made to care for anything or anyone. We are totally unreasonable.

Bloody uniforms are brought back from the front to be washed. Each of us is assigned to wash sixty shirts in lye. We cry. The lye, mixed with salty tears, is brutal on our hands. Liberation is unreasonable. We feel sorry for ourselves.

We realize that we are the only nonmilitary labor pool available to the Russians. Still, we are resentful. The Russians are good to us. They slaughter a cow and feed us on its flesh. We get huge amounts of meat. Still, there is no bread. There are no operating bakeries, no stores.

We loot in the nearby town of Prauschnitz. Regina organizes daily. The mother hen shops and shops for her brood.

Nothing is real, neither our restricted freedom nor our riches. We block Auschwitz from our minds and relish the evolving new era of chaotic order.

Where is Cipi?

HOPE IS
SHOUTING

AS MORE AND MORE areas in eastern Germany are liberated, the roads begin to yield survivors making their way on foot toward a railroad rumored to be in a town believed to be called Oelsk. Our village of Jagadschutz comes to life.

Hundreds of death-defiers begin to appear on the road. Isn't it strange? After all they have seen, lived through, suffered, known—they do not seem broken. They feed on insane kinds of hopes. So do we.

"Where do you come from?"

"Are you Hungarian? Polish? Italian?"

"Which camp were you in? For how long?"

"Did you escape, or was the camp liberated?"

"How many of your family survived?"

They march, and we shout questions at them. They keep shouting back.

"Did you know the Kleins from Kisvárda? The Weiszes from Miskolc? The Roths from Nyíregyháza? The Halperts from Hajdunánás?"

Names and descriptions fill the air. Hope is shouting everywhere.

"Have you seen Rosa or Sarah from Ajak?"

"Have you seen our sister Cipi?"

"How long have you been walking, marching?"

"Where are you going, and why?"

"Everybody is dead."

"No. No. No. My cousin found her sister yesterday. They say my uncle is alive. Rivka's cousin is supposed to be alive somewhere. Somebody heard it from somebody else, just yesterday."

The questions from us to the marchers, the questions from them to us, are irrepressible, constant. The marching language of hope is the sound of a new kind of after liberation symphony rising from the ashes of the Jews. There were seven in the Katz family, nine in the Gottesman, twelve in the Weisz. How many survived?

The refusal to accept the murder of our families, even after the stench of burning flesh that we know so well, and that stubborn smell of life on the road cannot be explained by anyone.

Who has had training enough in the humanities, in the mind-healing professions, in the emotional, philosophical, and literary terrain to be able to understand this mysterious insistence on life? Either the inward gazes, the depressed faces, and the dragging bodies are not too many, or we do not want to see them. Our eyes are stubborn. They search for life only. Intermittently there is a shriek because someone is told of someone's survival, because we recognize someone, or because we ourselves are recognized.

There is nothing inconsequential about the chaos that Hitler has wrought on these roads. It all deals with life, with death, with emotions, with love, with anxiety. Nothing is unmarred by what Hitler did; yet the mystery of humankind resurfacing seemingly unmarred cannot be fathomed. It is almost all there—feelings we used to have, curiosity about everything, love that we can feel, genuine kindness.

Can it all be true, or are we merely taking a hiatus from all that hate we were forced to endure, and coldness will seep into our hearts not long from now?

God, don't let that happen. This warm shower inside feels good, God. Let us be for a while, let us feel good for a bit. We are tired, God. Living in hate was very hard. Do you hear me, God? Living in hate was very hard.

There is a loving relationship between the road people and us. There is some possibility that maybe someone else in our family is alive. Every day, after our morning's cow work, Chicha, Regina, and I run to the road that draws us to it like a magnet of hope. We must find Philip, our brother. Philip, dear Philip, are you still alive?

Where is Cipi, our sister?

FROM TIME TO TIME it dawns on us that we have been detached from the rest of humankind. We will have to relearn how to live, how to hold a fork, how to live with the family of man. Too great a task. The resources within us will have to stand up to a nearly impossible struggle.

We have reverence for life, or no reverence at all. We have flare-ups of hope, or are dead within. We know almost everything about life or death. Still, we have to relearn how to walk, step by painfully fragile step. What will, what can, prop us up through these delicate inner negotiations?

A warring land is not without its share of decomposing bodies. They are strewn all around us. We step over them, devoid of any emotion. We no longer can locate the mourning niche for the dead in our shriveled souls.

We perk up only if some rags on the dead can be stolen, if something on the bodies is better than what we, the "living," are wearing.

Our training ground was Auschwitz. It is easy to step over the bodies on the roads of murder country. It is even easier when the bodies are clad in Nazi uniforms. Yet, whatever a body wears, parts of us are dead, and for moments we hurt from our inability to retrieve the heart or hurt of yesteryear. We want to cry not for the dead but for what is dead in us.

Will what we were return? A silent prayer is etched into our footsteps as we heartlessly step over a decomposing arm, a hip, or a head. Hitler's imprint is on the roads, in the sky, everywhere. He tore our insides into unbearable memories. He also set us up for hopes we should not have.

We try not to remember. We try not to think. Hitler, Hitler, why didn't you let us have normal deaths? Funerals? Tears? Why did you set us apart? Just graves, Hitler —we have survived into an age where a grave is a mark of humanity.

When we were growing up, our mothers and teachers taught us other values. The inspirations we were nurtured on were examples of humaneness. We read and wrote poetry of heroism, learned of a common goal for common man, of justice, of being in the service of common good, of becoming healers—doctors, nurses.

Our songs were love songs. We knew and felt tenderness. Were we misled by all who had a share in shaping us into young women and men? Is this the age of mockery, or were the years that sculpted us the mockery?

Hitler, we will forgive nothing you wrought. Even before you murdered us you tried to cripple our minds. We, the people of the Book, had to endure your book burnings. Knowledge in flames.

Some of us will forever weep for the books and schooling you denied us. The broken wings of our minds will always curse you for that. I curse you. So do Sally, Philip, Berta, Sam, Morris, Helen, Edith, Harry, Jacob, Nathan . . .

There is no peace on the roads, no peace in our hearts. Marchers, where are you marching? Step out of this age. Step off this planet. Life is tainted too much. Auschwitz is even bigger and more than whatever transpired before.

How will the world heal itself of Auschwitz? Is there a large pill for a large virus called hate? Is the world terminal? Can it get well? Can shattered lives ever be mended? Will saving the fragments be an impossible task?

All these unanswerable ponderings are floating about within our exhausted minds. They are not questions properly formed. They just take up chaotic residence within our souls.

VIGIL ON THE ROAD

OUR EYES are fixed on the road. We are trying desperately to refuel our sorrows with hope, baseless hope, but we are so desperate. How else can we hang on and clear our nostrils of that vile stench? We hug and hope anew when a lone voice yells out, "I am from Kisvárda. I had ten sisters and brothers. Parents, too. I am alone."

Chicha, Regina, and I were born there. We weep, and the lone one marches along.

The sun begins to fade on the cold afternoon. The marchers are fewer. The sun will rise in the morning on a denser group of hopers. Our feelings are sad and glad as we make our way back to the tending of the cows.

We still have to guard against rape, but no longer so fiercely. A more permanent core of Russian military personnel is now in place. We do not fear them. It is the movement of forces that is more threatening, but there is less of that now. The armed struggle to defeat the dying beast of Nazidom is farther and farther away from our temporary home.

We begin to accept the fact that we are the guardians of the cattle, that they would suffer hunger were we to not feed them. We cannot let that happen. We know about hunger. The odor of dung and hay is mixed now with the scent of burning flesh in our nostrils. The scent is better this way, more tolerable.

The bloody uniforms are no longer being brought back from the front. Our lives are better, and the road keeps pulling us with hope. It probably is wrong to hope this fervently, but what is there to do? We fantasize that tomorrow, the day after, or soon, Cipi will scream on the road, "Philip, look. Here they are!"

Yesterday passes, tomorrow passes, and soon passes, but the road refuses to yield the precious pair. Cipi and Philip must know that we are standing vigil on the road. Cipi, hurry. Philip, where are you?

Suddenly the road changes its look and its soul. We are riveted with frozen emotions. For the first time in all the years of war and venom, the victims, the vanquished, and the victors are together.

The Russians are leading an enormous number of captured German soldiers down the same road that conveyed the tortured ones, the dear ones, only yesterday. The footprints of love and hate are commingled in the dust, on the cement. This is the first time that we are facing the Nazis from a position of advantage. We are free and they are prisoners. A defeated body of killers, worn and bedraggled, is playing havoc with our tortured hearts.

What shall we do with them? Spit at them? Shout obscenities? Wish death on their children? Tell them that we would love to fill the sky with the smoke of burning flesh—theirs, and their mothers and infants, and their grandmothers and cousins, and their wives and friends, until they number six million?

What are we to do with all that is pent-up in our mending bodies, with our hideously altered memories, with the apocalypse in our heads, with all the pain of our

motherlessness? What are we to do now that we can begin to take revenge?

We are stunned with all that has crashed down on us
on the road. We are unprepared. We don't know how to
handle this good fortune that has suddenly come our
way.

We look at each other with ambivalence at this deci-
sive moment of truth. We know that something must ap-
pease the deep yearning for vengeance that has festered
for so long in our hearts. Rocks to smash their Nazi
heads, to splash the cells of their sick minds on the uniforms they were so proud to wear? We must do something, even if the Russians will punish us for it.

But, then, it must be awful to kill. We have never
killed before. We are paralyzed simply by contemplating
the thought. We are unable to do it. Yet we must do
something with our hate. We simply must.

We stoop to the roadbed, pick up some tiny pebbles,
and toss the pebbles at the Nazis.

LEARNING TO
LAUGH AGAIN

OUR KILLER INSTINCT subsides. We return to the road the following day to look for life.

The liberated keep walking, surging ahead toward the phantom train that will chug them home, where they stubbornly hope to find the missing members of their families. Some days, the crowds are thin; some days, massive.

We keep shouting, "Wherever you come from, have you seen our sister Cipi anywhere? Our brother's name is Philip. Philip Katz. Do you know if he is alive? Have you seen Cipi? Have you seen Philip? Do you know anyone who has? If you see them anywhere, tell them we are alive."

The road is fickle. It keeps betraying us. We are losing hope, but will not give up our dream of finding our sister and brother. We end our frustrating day by walking to a deserted nearby castle, which is frequently used by Red Army troops for overnight bivouac.

The castle ceilings are high enough to touch the heavens. The grand piano is covered with human feces. The bloody brown feathers of a freshly killed chicken decorate the keyboard. Revenge, apparently, can take any form.

We go to the castle for our "shopping" sprees. Looted as it is, the structure still yields wondrous things. One storage room contains built-in closets from floor to ceiling. Each closet is stocked with light bulbs of different sizes.

We need only one bulb but take an armful. Greed and revenge—neither will bring back our family, nor will it make the returning barons at war's end scrounge for bulbs. Still, it is good to know that there is shit on their piano. Let them smell the foul aroma while they listen to the music of that foul, anti-Semitic genius, Richard Wagner.

We don't move into the castle. We need no castles. We return to our original little home that was deserted by the German blacksmith who once lived there and chat with the three Polish girls about their love lives in our tiny palace of lust. We three Hungarian sisters and the Polish girls really belong to each other, for we are separated only in the knowing ways of sex. Our hearts and bodies were bruised by the same calamity. We sought freedom together, so we belong together.

We have been free for several weeks now. With the war farther and farther away from us, our inner chaos subsides somewhat. At intervals there is a modicum of peace in our heads. We are grateful for the ebbing rumblings.

We are settled into a curious routine, but just as we are beginning to feel a sense of stability, our anxiety returns. The cows, which we have resented and learned to care for, are suddenly to be taken away from us.

Everything, it seems, is constantly being taken from us.

The cattle are the only valuable commodity worth transporting anywhere. Where? To Russia? To milk them for the hungry children of that war-ravaged land? We don't know. We are ordered simply to get the cows to a collection point some distance from the barn and to do it immediately.

Inexperienced cowherds that we are, we begin to drive the cattle forward, using long wooden sticks as prods. We know absolutely nothing about the way such a task can be accomplished. We speak no cattle tongue and know no gestures that are intelligible to cows. Despite all our inane commands, the cattle go where they wish.

If we succeed in leading two cows forward, five turn and go backward. By the time we coax the five forward, the ones that were going ahead are on their way back. Now three of them are running sideways. Four forward. Two back again.

We yell. We plead. We cry. We swear. We promise the kingdom of heaven. But nothing we do, nothing we say keeps them moving straight ahead. They will not be ordered about, as if living in Hitler's barns has affected them, too.

There are dozens of cows, and each seems to have a mind of its own. The sun is shining. Our task is ridiculous. We haven't smiled for an eternity. Suddenly all hell breaks loose in us. We start to laugh hysterically. Chicha wields her stick and laughs. Regina pursues a cow and laughs. I fall on the ground and laugh.

We laugh and joke. For all the world we are the happiest cattle herders in this rotten land. The cows do as they wish, while all that is pent up in us explodes in crazy, joyous laughter.

Finally, we calm down and make a determined effort to regiment our charges. We succeed in driving the cattle a little farther ahead. Then the scene repeats itself. We gain an inch, we lose ten. We try again. We howl some more. The sun has set. It is getting late and cool. At last, we deliver the independent creatures to their destination.

With a job so well done, we return to our modest quarters and recount each scene amid new waves of laughter. We know now that we still can have fun, even if it takes a herd of cattle to make it happen. We are happy that we have relearned how to laugh.

LEARNING TO CRY

WE WILL HAVE to learn how to cry. . . .

But if we let the tears flow, how long would we weep? For all eternity? For six million years?

The cows are gone. Now there is no basic food supply from anywhere. The available food in the area keeps diminishing. Only the people absolutely necessary for managing things will be permitted to remain. The others will have to move on. They will have to try to make their way to their various homelands.

We hope that the war will soon be won and trains will become available. We have consumed everything edible. Food that is scarce cannot be divided fairly. It is clear that we will have to leave.

The Russians provide us with some kind of discharge papers, attesting to our work record, or whatever. They seem regretful and honorable, but it doesn't satisfy us. We want to remain. Our minds understand that we must leave, but our emotions react in a deeply wounded way. In our hearts, we feel that the curse of the wandering Jew is upon us again.

THE DECEPTION

WE ARE DESPERATE. We do not want to give up the relative security of what we have here. For six weeks we have had some kind of home. Diabolical, ironic that we should consider as something good an abandoned house in this vile land.

It is still cold and wintry. We know that no one is waiting for us at home in Hungary. If Cipi and Philip are alive, they know that, too. If ever we can go anywhere, we will go to America, to New York, to our father, our only living parent.

We love being liberated. We think of the Russian soldiers as life-givers. They kept the Germans from annihilating us. They are responsible for our reentering life. They let no dogs loose on us. They let no Dr. Mengele loose on us. Their smoke emits the smell of food, not the scent of burning flesh.

Now they are imploring us to leave. When we procrastinate, they order us to go.

"We need more healing."

"Food is scarce. Can't you see that?"

"Yes, but we are afraid. Let us stay a little longer."

Our pleas are to no avail. We must leave, like all the

others. We will join the road people until we find a train that will deliver us to a land of peace.

Where is that land of peace? How long are we to wander before we can cry ourselves to sleep on our own pillows?

We organize and organize until we accumulate a heap of clothes. What to sort out, what to take on this, our new unknown journey? What will be warm enough to fend off the cold, light enough to carry, strong enough to protect us?

The last time we made such decisions, we found ourselves at journey's end in the cannibal kingdom of Auschwitz. Where will this journey lead?

We are glum, contemplative. Our last march, the death march, is still burned into the soles of our feet. We look for an image of solace and come to rest on the hope that while on the road, we might bump into the missing members of our family.

We find a small wagon on which to load our belongings. We load items, remove them, put them back again. It is so difficult to part with any of our newfound riches. Our wagon, we know, must not be overburdened. We will have to pull it wherever we go, and our trip may be long and wearisome. We choose, discard, reacquire. We have a special fondness for a large robe. It is dark red with white checks. It is too heavy, but we pile it on the wagon.

Slowly we make peace with the prospect of living a road life. There will be, we pray, compensating factors. We say good-bye to those who remain, knowing well that we will never share good or bad again, and join the multinational, multilingual remnants of the bloodbath.

Almost immediately we begin to make friends and share the tales of common horrors.

"Which camp were you in? How many were in your family? How many survived? Who are you looking for? Do you have any hope?"

We talk and walk. We walk and remember. We walk and hurt. We wipe away tears that haven't surfaced yet. Sometimes we hum tunes.

Each day, as dusk approaches, we look for deserted homes to sleep in, homes that lodged yesterday's travelers. This kind of life calls for intuition and ingenuity. We have to share, be compassionate, crowd together, grab, run before others get there. Some villages yield an abundance of empty homes, others only a scant few.

We are helpful and kind to one another. The food we have brought along keeps us well. We keep walking during daylight, settle before dark.

On the third night we find shelter in a room with two large mattresses on the floor. A middle-aged woman joins us to share our "beds." She keeps talking about her twin daughters who were separated from her by Dr. Mengele upon their arrival at Auschwitz. She insists that her daughters are alive. Her faith in their survival is like a religious fervor.

We are skeptical, but we haven't the heart to tell her otherwise. We know that Mengele's particular passion was to perform medical experiments on twins.

We prepare for bed. Regina and I take one mattress, Chicha and the woman the other. Suddenly, a drunken soldier enters the room. He sizes up the situation and chooses a bedmate. *"Chornaya,"* he mutters, selecting Chicha, my dark-haired sister. He quickly undresses and turns out the light.

In the dark the middle-aged woman switches places with Chicha.

In the morning the soldier realizes the deception. He

smiles, dresses, and departs. On his way out he tosses a gold watch to his most recent conquest. The woman becomes part of our wandering family.

Finally, we lose her on the road, and much later we learn that she has actually, miraculously, found her twins alive in Budapest.

On our journey the woman never stopped talking about her children. She was certain the gods had decreed that somewhere another mother would give her body to a drunken soldier, as she had done, to save her daughters' virginity. We shall always remember her faith. We do not remember her name.

DISSOLVE
THE ROAD

OUR TROUBLES seem to be lessening. From here on, no attempts are made to violate our bodies. The farther away we get from the gruesome face of war, the less often do the soldiers around us bury themselves in alcohol.

Now we try to converse with the Russians. We speak no Russian at all, except for the few words that ruled our lives while we were cow-tending: *"Nyet raboty, nyet khleba"*—"No work, no bread." Those words, literally, were our daily bread. We had no right, we were told, to expect unearned food; everyone must work. The Russian words were enough to spur us on to earn our food.

Upon passing through the gates at Auschwitz, we were confronted with the Nazi slogan *"Arbeit macht frei"*— "Work makes one free." The German words offered no nourishment, no spur, only freedom to work.

Whoever passed through those gates was treated to more "freedom" than any mind is capable of conjuring up. Remembrance of the vile Nazi slogan, the insidious invitation to labor, the sick mockery, forces my eyes shut even decades later. By comparison, the Russian slogan was a lilting song of praise to human dignity.

With body gestures we now address the Russians. We

communicate the fact that we do not speak their language.

"All right, so you can't *speak* our language, but surely you can *understand* it?"

The Russian logic makes us laugh.

The barrier of language becomes an enemy amid the desire for friendship between the liberators and the liberated. How strange that war can be funny, too.

The kilometers shrink while they seem endless. Our energies are ebbing. Is there no resting place for human beings as weary as we are? With each step our wagon seems to be heavier and harder to pull. We agonize over each treasure we are forced to eliminate.

Were we always walking? Were we born walking? Where is the end of the road? We are tired of dragging the whole of our lives in this stinking country of destruction.

We are still in Germany. We cannot walk fast enough to leave it behind forever. We would like to dissolve the road, for this is Hitler's *Reich*. We want to leap over this contaminated ground, swim the Atlantic to the New World, and cleanse ourselves of the hate of Hitler in that great big body of water.

Each day the rising sun finds us on the road. Nearly till sunset, we walk in search of an elusive train. The bonds we cement en route have a built-in component—loss. For a long time now, only loss seems to mark love. We touch, emotions engage, then disengage again. All the marchers are bound for different countries, different lives, and all have common memories of pain.

Our truest search is for love, reentanglement with those we loved. Everything is altered. All the road walkers want is to protect their own. But for most of them there is no one to protect. They walk alone.

We are fortunate. There are three of us. There were more. They are no more. Hope flickers and fades. Perhaps there will never be more, only the three of us and our father, if he is still alive in that far-off world of America.

Our father is all alone. What are his dreams? Does he lull himself to sleep with unrealities? By now he must know the truth—that Dr. Mengele devastated his people, that all of his family could not still be alive. How does he live? Does God help him?

We have grown so far from our father. The cruelest time, we spent apart. If ever we see him, how should we greet him?

"Hello, Father. We are alive. They are not."

How long have we been marching? Our aching legs know the answer—many days, perhaps a week. It is the month of March now.

March 1945 has nothing in common with the Marches we used to know. March used to be springtime; falling-in-love time; old-fashioned, romantic, serenading time; leisure-walk time, up and down Main Street, in Kisvárda, Hungary.

It was a time when I really didn't have to take a little mirror from my purse to fix my hair. My hair didn't need fixing. I just pretended. I just wanted to see in the mirror's reflection whether that tall, lanky, newest fancy of mine was following me. My tiny town held all the wonders of the world for me—life, death, love.

Our steady, wearying journey now affords me a steady stream of time for contemplation. And I keep remembering.

· REMEMBERING

THERE ARE SIX young people in my home: my four sisters, my one brother, myself. Our ages range from thirteen to twenty-something. If God made all of us in His image, God must be filled with love of life, sizzling excitement, and curiosity.

We girls try on my aunt's large bra with nothing to fill it. We squabble. We make up.

Boys flock to our house. "Is Philip home?"

Liars!

They have come to check whether the five pairs of developing young bosoms have grown firmer, the hips rounder, the curves more graceful. They have come to tease and pinch and touch.

We make believe the boys are really friends of our brother. We are liars, too. We want them to look. We want them to feel.

Later they come to our home as young men, lying less, reaching gently for an arm to caress, lips to kiss, hair to smooth; engaging in the virginal games of the sexually restricted forties. The boys are there all the time, winter and summer.

In the winter we huddle together in front of our tall, tile, heating unit, which we feed continually with wooden logs. The radio blasts ugly news and delicious music. We move close to each other and gaze at the fire. We seek comfort from that other fire raging in the atmosphere. That other fire makes us shiver. That other fire has an icy name called Hitler.

We try to muffle Hitler's crackling with singing. We are forever singing the popular songs of the day.

Sándor drums away with his fingers and knuckles. He is a natural percussionist, using any chair in range as his musical instrument. He sings. He dances. From moment to moment he seizes one of us five girls and tangos around the kitchen table.

Lacy plays cards. Miki tells jokes. Harry philosophizes.

Cipi rouges her cheeks. Regina braids her hair. Potyo licks honey from the honey jar.

Chicha writes poetry. Philip teaches Hebrew to his friends in the attic. I adjust my skirt and respond to a call for another dance.

My mother waits for a letter from America, from my father, and worries about Hitler.

We argue about politics, fight for first place in my mother's heart, and call her a pessimist. We put on snowshoes and, in groups of five, six, or seven, go out for romantic midnight strolls in the snow-covered, frozen world of Kisvárda.

Afterward we play dominoes, dance another dance, sing another song, and say good night. We stay up very late, extending time, for our lives may be short.

In the summer we no longer go to the Carpathian Mountains, so we tan ourselves bronze in our war-clouded backyard. We pour buckets of water on each other from the ever-full barrel of rainwater outside our house. We spend much time frolicking at home—our courtyard has had to replace our Carpathian vacation land.

Kazi lives at the other end of our yard. I am in love with him. His balcony is higher than mine. He can look down on me. I can look up to him. We have looked at each other for years, but we have never actually met. We would have had to meet formally, and we couldn't. We come from totally different worlds.

Hungary is a fiercely anti-Semitic country. I am a middle-class Jewish girl, Kazi an aristocratic gentile. If friendship between two such different people can exist, it has to be in a large city where people can submerge their identities without notice. Kisvárda is a very small town, too small for things so large, so complex. So I just love Kazi from afar.

I spend endless hours on my balcony, looking up at his balcony while he looks down at me. Kazi is tall, blond, lean, strong. Kazi is beautiful.

We love and never meet. We love and never talk. We love and never touch.

What happened to you, Kazi? Could you, too, have been an anti-Semite? And, if so, why did I love you, Kazi?

Chicha, did I, too, love your boyfriend Gyuszi? I don't remember. I only remember the pain I felt when I saw you cry, when news of his death came. You couldn't stop crying.

The Germans had used him as a human "mine detector" on the Russian front. They forced him, as well as other Jewish slaves, to walk across open fields in advance of German tanks. When he stepped on a hidden mine, his small body and large eyes were blown into smithereens.

Was there a face more beautiful and a pen more poetic? You held on to his poems as though adoring a god. And you wrote poetry to him when there was no Gyuszi anymore. Chicha, did you ever again love anyone the way you loved him?

I must stop remembering. I must keep walking into the future, with blisters forming on my feet, in this ugly, foreign land.

I must stop remembering . . .

THE TERRITORY
OF MY MIND

OUR BLISTERS hurt. However urgent the future, we must rest for a day. We say good-bye to our week-old friends of the road. We will join the next group of future-pursuers on the morrow.

Immediately, I forget my determination not to remember, and I think of my mother. I hear her voice again: "Hitler will lose the war, children, but he will win it against the Jews."

I remember my mother's extraordinary social consciousness, her involvement with the fate of mankind. My mother could barely squeeze her vision into the narrow confines of our age. Her mind was bursting with the largeness of the future. The twentieth century was too narrow and too cruel for her.

We were the young people in our home, but my mother was the embodiment of what the spirit of youth should be. Her physical needs were modest, but her expectations from the human species were immodest and visionary. What haunted her was the fear that human beings might fail to measure up to their potential.

On that ugly ride in the cattle car that delivered her into Mengele's inferno, she had an unforgettable look of hope and prayer for her children, combined with total resignation about the days left for her. She didn't know about Auschwitz, as none of us knew, but she knew that something horrendous would be the culmination of that insane journey.

How could she have known about Auschwitz? In our anti-Semitic, Nazi-sympathizing country, there was no negative publicity about Hitler and his deeds. The German *Führer* ranted of glory, not of Auschwitz, over Hungary's airwaves.

Filthy Jews! Heil Hitler! Jews! Jews! Heil Hitler!

Those were the deafening sounds thundering out of Hungary's radio. The fascist lies that were spewed forth spoke of Hitler, the *Ubermensch,* not of German crematoriums. The Jews had no special envoys whispering the real truth in their ears. Jews knew only what Hitler and his henchmen wanted them to know.

And had we known what was happening, what could we possibly have done? The world was not clamoring or rallying to save us. We were utterly alone, unorganized, and unarmed—children, women, the old, the sick; our able-bodied men had been taken away from us as slave laborers years ago. When the trained armies of every European country had fallen before the German beasts, could we weak civilian remnants have fought the Nazis with our shoelaces, our spoons, our pencils?

I squint my eyes in agony as the road seems to narrow in the distance. In the past few weeks thousands have walked this way. Their life-affirming steps echo a legacy of encouragement to those who follow. But my pain and anger keep intruding, however hard I try to fix my gaze on the road that is supposed to deliver me into the future.

History is tugging at my head. It invades the entire inner territory of my mind. If freedom is inner, then I am not free. I never will be. We are walking in a country that violated everything free men ever stood for, violated even our ability to enjoy freedom, for it imprisoned our memories in a permanent, hideous way. I am sure that we will try to break free, but the images in our heads are so powerful, they probably will not respond to the healing of time; they probably will be our companions until we die.

Our flesh seems to have responded better. Almost immediately after our escape, we began to put on weight. We forced insane amounts of food into our hardly used stomachs. We abused our bellies pitifully; nonetheless, we grew stronger, fatter, and healthier with each mouthful. Whatever ailed us, we medicated with food. The food made us both ill and well.

It is so wonderful to see the contours and adornments of our bodies again—bosoms, head hair, underarm hair, pubic hair. The human beings on the road no longer look like *Muselmanns,* like walking skeletons. That is all we were used to seeing, except for the attack dogs and the Nazi dogs. We seem to have been on a journey to a bizarre planet, and now we are back again. Will we be allowed to conclude our insane journey and be able to die in bed? An image of children surrounding the bedside of a dying parent is so comforting. Will we ever reach that stage of comfort?

The roads are alive with seemingly large numbers of people, but in comparison to those who were murdered, they are but a handful. The marchers are not only the survivors of the death camps, but others, too—partisans, freed political prisoners, Jews who had been hiding for years with false identity papers, liberated Allied soldiers from around the globe, and, probably, some Nazis in disguise, mingling in our midst as victims, seeking to escape retribution.

We are unable to weed the Nazis out, and wonder whether any authority anywhere will ever be able to cut through their false papers, their fairy tales, their lies. Some, no doubt, will be unmasked; most, probably, will not. Will they sit next to me on a bus in a far-off land someday? In America? Will they live on the same street where I am nurturing my children? Will Dr. Mengele breathe the same air as my family? The thought is shattering. Will the Nazis, with altered features, live happily and commingle with us in a grocery store, in a theater?

We wore yellow stars to single us out.

What will they wear?

FORGED IN FIRE

WE ARE STILL in Germany, marching toward a magic train that will take us away from here. German pebbles hurt our feet—and everything else. We vow never to set foot here again. With each step, we are nearer the blessed train, but not near enough to feel peaceful. Peace might come, perhaps, when we inhale the smoke of the locomotive. Wearily we trudge on, till the end of day, to start anew in the morning.

Almost two weeks have passed since we left Jagadschutz on foot. The war has not yet ended, but we are certain now that it will. In a sense it has ended for us. We are beyond the reach of the Nazis. Their struggle with the Russians and the Allies is far enough to the rear for us not to worry. The Germans are not about to return.

We are now at the outskirts of a town whose name, we learn, is Oelsk, or something that sounds like Oelsk. No town has a greater lure, for, incredibly, there are railroad tracks leading into it.

Soon a train is within view.

A vision of that other train, a train of crowded cattle cars and death, appears in my head. I force the image from my mind and conjure up another vision, a childhood memory of a choo-choo train bearing my mother, my grandmother, and the six of us children to the Carpathian Mountains for a summer vacation. Did we really have a childhood, or were we always prisoners? I try to ease the pain of the present, but it doesn't really work. We are where we are. We are where we have been, lugging a few rags we can discard and a mammoth monster we cannot—Auschwitz. It was there that we were sewn together emotionally. It is that oneness, forged in fire, love tended to in such a place of hate, that perhaps led us to escape from the death march and on to this life march.

I look at my sisters and remember their acts of goodness, their fear and bravery. I remember how Regina donned an armor of fearlessness right after liberation to conceal her terror. She stuck a knife in one boot and announced, "No one will ever harm me again!"

She has not parted with the knife, nor has she had to use it. Could she if she had to?

We draw strength from this young avenger. I look at her with loving prayers. May no harm come to this child, God. She has suffered so much. She must have some laughter still tucked away in her. Her sense of humor used to keep us sane throughout the difficult years. She stopped laughing in Auschwitz.

I look at Chicha in awe. She is indomitable, the most faithful replica of my mother, reflecting my mother's resolute vision of a better age. Is Chicha's faith justified? Can a faith so abused save itself? I look at her pleadingly for an answer. Help me restore my faith, Chicha. Why is your faith not more shaken? Where do you get it?

You are so small of frame, Chicha. You are so big, damn it! How could you have shared the way you did in Auschwitz, where there was nothing to share, save suffering? How could you have said, "I really am not hungry," and given me a morsel of your morsel? I couldn't have done it. You, like me, weighed no more than forty or fifty pounds. Yet you were able to say, "I am not hungry."

Will mothers like ours and daughters like you save the soul of humankind? What would the world, littered with inhumanity, be without a few like you? We need those like you to help us heal the Earth.

Perhaps it is worth living, after all.

MANYI

I MUST THINK of goodness, else I cannot go on. I reach for my friend Manyi in my mind.

Manyi was working in the *Unterkunft* at the time we arrived at Auschwitz. The *Unterkunft* was the temporary hoarding place, the warehouse, for all the fine things we brought along from our homes and which were confiscated by the Nazis upon our arrival.

The stolen possessions and clothing had to be sorted in the warehouse before shipment to the good people of that good Germany. The *Unterkunft* was an isolated building with pleasant living quarters for the Nazi in charge. For his personal comfort the Nazi needed a maid, a cook, and whatever else—and Manyi was that maid and cook and whatever else.

Manyi was kept well fed, not like us. She looked like an actual woman. She was beautiful and good. That "whatever else" enabled her not only to live, but also to get me and several other girls jobs sorting clothes. Those jobs had very small, but very important, benefits.

Each time we entered or left the *Unterkunft*, we were frisked. At times, however, at great risk, it was possible to sneak out a knife or other small item in our shoes to barter for a crumb of bread from a miserable creature out in the camp. A prisoner with a knife had the possibility of self-deception. She could slice her wretched portion of "daily bread," a mixture of flour and sawdust, into paper-thin slices, thus making it appear to be more than it really was and enabling the slices to be apportioned for the day.

The apportionment, however, like the slicing, didn't work. It was impossible to maintain the self-deception for long. We were too hungry.

"I will save this slice for the afternoon, that one for the evening."

Such promises could not be kept. The torture of eyeing the slices, touching them, and pulling the hands back again was intolerable. We touched a slice and stole the corner. We touched again and stole again. Thus, we kept stealing our own hard-earned bread.

When I got desperately ill with typhus and couldn't report to work, Manyi sneaked Chicha into the *Unterkunft* in my stead. Such a breach of the "holy" Nazi rules could have cost Manyi her life, or, at the least, her "whatever else" job. The job was important to her, both for her own sake and for what it enabled her to do to help her fellow prisoners. Not that she had a choice about her fate; she had none—she was chosen to kiss the depraved, and relatively few were chosen for this dubious honor.

Is a lice-filled bag of bones a woman, an object of desire? With the exception of a few—people working in the kitchens, *Kapos,* the handful of women singled out for German lust—we all were just such bags of bones. Can anyone imagine a lice-filled walking skeleton as a goddess of love?

Manyi, good Manyi, you should have lived. Your beastly Nazi lover, your lover of hate, should have died.

I am free now. Why do I keep harking back to that terrible terrain again and again? Are those memories forever encased within me and I shall never be free?

Someone, please, tear my inner dungeon and let me out. I want to be free. It is close to springtime. Let me smell the flowers, inhale the perfume of earth's creations, not Dr. Mengele's stench.

I want to be free, Doctor. You controlled me in your gruesome prison. Don't control my freedom. I want you dead not only in reality, but in memory, too. I want you excised from all of us. When will that be? In which millennium? Once and for all, will I ever be able to say, "Good-bye, Dr. Mengele?"

I probably won't last out this century. Will our children be able to forget what we shall tell them? Will we have the heart to tell them what we know? We will have to, because history cannot be trusted. It distorts. Will anyone believe the unbelievable?

We are within inches of the train in Oelsk as my mind pokes and probes. We can touch the train. It is not made up of cattle cars. It is a crazy, wonderful train with regular cars, with bunklike arrangements for sleeping, with a huge cauldron of food being mixed by a rosy-cheeked woman soldier of the Russian Army. She has the kindly, smiling face of a heavy mama. Nourish us, dear mama. We are still very hungry.

Will our hunger ever subside enough to enable us to order a normal meal in a restaurant? Will we ever use a fork and knife, or will we always gobble? Will I ever be able to mix food with conversation, put down my fork long enough to finish a sentence? Do people talk at mealtime, or do they eat, eat, eat?

Hail to food. I have no time to talk.

As a young girl in my hometown of Kisvárda, Hungary.

A year before deportation.

My family: back row *from left:* Chicha, me, Philip, Cipi, Regina; front row: Potyo, Mother.

My brother Philip, wearing the compulsory yellow star; Kisvárda ghetto, 1944.

3 Survivors of German Death Camps
Begin New Life in 'Wonderful U. S.'

'THIS WONDERFUL AMERICA' — The United States is a dreamland, say these three sisters, all survivors of Auschwitz, ill-famed German prison camp. Left to right, Regina Katz, Mrs. Jack Berman and Isabella Katz. — Photo by The Binghamton Press

This appeared in the *Binghamton Press* soon after our arrival in America.

SELF-PORTRAIT 1945

Isabella Weither (I signed my name in 1983)

PRISON NO. 792/2

This portrait of despair, drawn soon after my arrival in
1945, is flecked with red; according to psychiatrists, the red
reflects an ever-present life force.

Adjusting to new life in America.

At a New York
concert hall in 1948.

When I came to America, no one could fathom Auschwitz. Desperate to release the flood of feelings and emotions inside me, I began writing in Hungarian on whatever scraps of paper were available, in restaurants, at home, whenever the urge overcame me. Decades later, these scraps formed the basis of my first book, *Fragments of Isabella*. This piece became the beginning of the book: "Yesterday, what happened yesterday . . ."

As a wife and mother, 1980.
I had defeated Hitler's design
to exterminate the entire Jewish
people. I survived, and today
two beautiful sons call me
Mother.

My son Richard, 1984.

My son Peter, 1977.

With my husband
Irving, in the
Grand Tetons,
1989.

With Irving, Richard, and Peter in St. Petersburg,
Russia, at the world premiere of Irving's play,
Isabella, based on *Fragments of Isabella*, May 8, 1993.

THE TRAIN
TO ODESSA

WE BEGIN TO CLIMB aboard the train, we and the others, the dear others from around the globe: Jews who weren't murdered, and liberated soldier prisoners, soldiers who killed in order to stop Hitler from murdering us. Tall Englishman, short Hindu, blond Scot, smiling American, Palestinian Jew, Sino-European, Czech Jewess, French fighter, people from tiny hamlets and great nations—and three Jewish girls from Kisvárda, Hungary. All these, plus the Russian soldiers responsible for our journey and our liberation.

Our commonality is overwhelming. We are all survivors of the same disease, hate. In this moving venture we nourish each other with care and concern. There is no common language between us, yet we speak the same tongue. With the touch of a hand, a comforting gesture, a look, we understand each other's recent past.

Those who are returning to their homes and families seem fully to comprehend that we three—Regina, Chicha, and I—and the other liberated Jewish survivors are a breed separate and apart. No one will be brewing coffee, serving drinks, baking bread and cookies for us at the end of our journey, wherever that end will be. Families will not be waiting for us; no one will be sitting around listening to our war stories. Our mothers and fathers did not accumulate letters from us while we were gone. There will be no parties to celebrate our kind of heroism. There will be no music and no neighbors weeping with joy for us, no tears for our dead.

Wherever we go, we will be alien orphans. Home is nowhere for us—not in our native land, not in any new land that will have us. We will have to learn a new language, a new culture, a new mode of dress and behavior. We will have to learn to control the rage inside us or make peace with it. We will have to learn how to communicate the unbelievable or keep silent and make believe that we just happened upon this side of the ocean or the other.

In this train we have an identity: We are little girls from a big war. On the other side of the ocean, should we ever reach that haven, we will be the strangest of strangers, from a continent of killing that contained within it yet other continents called Auschwitz and Bergen-Belsen and other strange names.

The Hindu sits in the lotus position and never talks. Does he ever sleep? It doesn't seem so. The Czech Jewess falls in love with the tall Englishman. The Palestinian promises the blessings of the kibbutz, the whole kibbutz, to Regina. The New Zealander promises New Zealand to Chicha. And Les, the dearest, gentlest, American soldier, mothers me with the most exquisite sensitivity.

Les is about twenty-two, but he adopts me as though I were an infant in need of ceaseless care. He must have seen Auschwitz or some other death camp, for he looks at me in total awe. In his every move he seems determined to somehow make up for the ferocious crime committed against me.

For two weeks, as the train rolls toward Odessa, Les seems to suspend his own person so that all he has, all he is, can be put in the service of healing. I don't think he is in love with me—he *is* love, total love. He provides something warm for my shoulders, something cool to quench my thirst, something nourishing to make me gain weight. Where does he get it all?

Each time the train stops, Les disappears and comes back with the sweetest balms. His delicacy is so unique that everyone is touched by it. Never have I seen such gentleness, as if some mysterious force willed the antithesis of Auschwitz upon me. Les asks for nothing in exchange.

I wonder now, so many years later, how much that young American was able to glean from my awe of him, from the depth of my loving appreciation, from my loving gratitude.

For two weeks the train keeps stopping in all kinds of places for all kinds of intervals. We visit with the other riders; by now, we all feel like kin. We do not understand the logistics of travel in a war-torn land. Are the frequent stops necessary for the movement of more urgent cargo in the other direction? Ammunition? Guns? The war is still in progress. It is March 1945. When will the war end? Are there concentration camps still to be liberated? Is Cipi in one of them? Is Philip?

War is noisy as hell, but it is silent concerning its secrets. It is so hard to find out anything. Gossip of great victories abounds. We love the stories. Are they true? Will the war be over soon?

The train is very long. Masses of people are riding on it, but we have all been on board for so long that to us it is a traveling community. Food is available or not. The motherly Russian cook concocts a magic all-in-one meal whenever she gets a delivery of ingredients from who-knows-where. In her huge cauldron she stirs vegetables and meat with a giant wooden spoon. We watch her prepare the "family meal" with delicious excitement. If only food were cooking around the clock . . . but it is not.

On some days we are terribly hungry. We talk about nothing but food. We are frustrated by the British. They alone seem to be different. They do not complain. They talk about the weather, the dog that runs past the train, the countryside—anything but food. Were they not to eat for a year, it seems, they would not complain. They are stony-faced at the mention of food. What makes them the way they are? Why can't they say they are hungry?

In certain villages the train stops long enough for us to go to the open farmers' markets, which are filled with the aroma of the morning's harvest. The peasants are kindly, but we have no money. We hardly remember what money looks like.

The peasants have food but lack clothing. We barter our stockings and other items from the "wardrobe" we dragged along from the blacksmith's house. Some peasants want our stockings more than anything else. We do not understand why. We barter with them for eggs and return to our train home.

In a battered pan, Regina collects scalding water droplets from the steam plumes of the locomotive. We keep the eggs in the hot water long enough to half cook them, then enjoy a sumptuous feast; we are happy again.

We roll along and stop again. We barter for potatoes and cook them in an instant fireplace of burning twigs.

They are tastier, it seems, than any dish that any gourmet chef could prepare. Our battered pan is lovable and lickable whenever sticky food graces its contours.

We are happy with our lot, with our train, with our companions. The Russian cook is cooking again. We love her food. We love her.

At each stop, romance is refueled. We roll cigarettes and stroll flirtatiously in the sun. Our hair has grown a bit. We can actually begin to use a comb. We have not had any use for one in nearly a year. It is an uncanny sensation.

We stroll beside the train displaying our short crowns of an inch of hair. With our newly found womanhood, we attract the attention of the men of our world. We are our very attractive selves again, and the soldiers on our train admire us, are ready to whisk us away to cities and hamlets we have never heard of.

But our plans are different. We have yet to search, to find parts of our old family before we try to create a new one. Our yearnings are fixed on what was: Cipi, Philip, my father.

Innocent, global flirtations en route to Odessa are such fun, but we are on our way to America, not Australia, New Zealand, or India. We are looking for Kisvárda. We will go all the way to America to try to find it. We are not in love yet, only intrigued by the very real possibility that someday we will be.

As I sit on the train, Les sensitively bandages my inner wounds. Chicha and Regina report on new conquests. "I was proposed to," says Chicha. "So was I," says Regina.

All a beautiful thing has to do is get off the train for a walk and she gets a marriage proposal. However playful and unserious these promises of heaven are, they nurture the long-dead womanhood in us, and we are grateful to these Don Juans of a devastating war. May you never war again, handsome soldiers. May this train, with its gathering of exiles, travel into an age of peace. We are all so tired.

IS THERE ANY PLACE TO STROLL?

THE TRAIN pulls into a large railroad station. It is Lemberg. A moment of affection for Lemberg: It is the city of an old family friend.

The early spring day turns cool. People around the station pull their clothing closer to their bodies. Everything —the station, the weather, the people—looks gray.

An enormous number of gapers are idling about. They seem jobless, purposeless, tired of the war. They, like us, are liberated. Why does the air around them feel so heavy, so overwhelmed with defeat?

As we have done at many stops, we get off the train for our exploratory stroll, eager for life-affirming scenes, sounds, gestures, words. Suddenly, we are assaulted by a repressed, staccato hiss: *Jews! Jews! Jews!* Sullen townspeople in our path are spewing their hatred at us.

Whoever wants to stroll, don't stroll in Lemberg. Don't stroll where the residue of hate mars the night in March. Don't stroll where people know not when to stop. Don't stroll in "never-enough" places.

Is there any place to stroll?

We are frightened and run back to the love we have come to know on the train. As the train pulls out, we cry thick, unwipeable tears. The liberated soldiers with us, who fought against just this kind of hatred, are angry enough to want to shoot again. We want to run to the outer perimeters of this world and leap over to another.

The train is too slow. We want to reach a safer town. Is there one? Everyone around us is sad and frustrated. They comfort us with compassion mixed with anger. They do what they can to ease our pain, realizing that the good battle is not yet over. Perhaps it never will be.

Regina, Chicha, and I draw close to each other. We remember too much at the very time we desperately want to learn the art of forgetting. Full of sadness, we drop off to sleep. When we awake, we are reassured by the gentle smiles of our guardians. We are out of Lemberg.

When next we stop, our steps are less nimble as we alight from the train. We inch our way with caution and are happy to sense neither love nor hate. We try to force Lemberg out of our fragile, wounded hearts. At each subsequent stop, we gain more confidence. We recover our spirit, begin to smile, and show off our aliveness. Look, everybody: We didn't let them kill us.

The train huffs and puffs to its destination. Each time it whistles, it heralds the arrival of the live ones, the ones who dared to outlive Hitler.

A meager lunch is served in a cheerful place in the next town. There are napkins on the table. To us the service seems almost elegant. Still, we gobble down our food while the English fuss with the proprieties of "dining." Leisurely and time-consumingly, they ceremoniously lift their forks with the left hand, cut tiny portions with the right hand, and chew minuscule bites. We don't understand.

At another stop, we see a hefty Russian woman operating a crane. The sight of the woman in such a masculine job is new to us. We marvel at her efficiency and are amused by this unfamiliar reversal of roles. Suddenly, the woman cups her hands in front of her mouth and yells, "Do you have silk stockings? I'll give you rubles in exchange."

We find a pair, and the woman's smudged face lights up. We complete the transaction and joyfully speculate about the food we will purchase at the next marketplace.

The Russian woman puts her arm into the stockings, looking for imperfections, then lovingly folds and tucks them into her bosom. Feeling like capitalists, we count and fondle our rubles. Then, because we have neither purses nor pockets, we, too, tuck our treasure into our bosoms.

Such a colorful, bartering journey is not likely to be repeated on trips we shall take in our civilized life to come. But right now we are truly enjoying this upside-down joyride as a funny, twisted gift of war.

Our spirits are healthy on the train for a variety of reasons, but the prime one has to be that this dearest of trains is delivering us out of a land of shame. In Germany we couldn't clear our lungs. The oxygen we inhaled there felt like a disease. Living needs fresh air. Germany emitted an air of death.

For our new life we must cross the ocean. We must put the cleansing waters of the sea between us and where we have been. It is true that disease can spread from country to country, but perhaps it cannot cross the ocean. I conjure a vision of great white waves blocking my view of Germany. I hear the roaring sea drowning out the roars of evil memory: *Heil, Hitler! Heil, Hitler!*

Now the train, with its sounds of deliverance, comes to rest in a big Russian city, and we are invited for a big

treat. We are lined up for a long walk through bombed-
out neighborhoods. It is a city sizzling with life. Clearing
of rubble is going on everywhere to the blaring sounds of
news and music emanating from a public address system.
The thunder of rousing military marches invigorates our
steps as we arrive at a huge farm.

The Russians guide us through the technological wonders of a "modern" farm. We detect their pride, even as
we do not comprehend their language. Most of us are
not interested in their latest agricultural machinery, but
we feel like dancing at the sight of the generous farm-
fresh spread they have prepared for us.

Thank you, Russians. Thank you for liberating us.
Thank you for the food. Good luck with your harvest.
There is friendship and laughter. With our stomachs deliciously full, we practically dance our way back to our
train.

ODESSA

WE DON'T KNOW what Odessa will bring. Our emotions are scrambled. We know that our newfound friends will soon scatter, and the gentleness and love we were nourished on during these past two weeks will seep out of our lives. The cuddling comfort we felt will dissipate in the reality of separation.

We spend the last few hours of our long train odyssey jotting down names and addresses. We have no location to give, unless our father is still alive at 166 Ross Street. We make promises of lifelong loyalty, of remembering, knowing full well that distances and time tend to erode promises.

Still, it is good to know that in a far-off corner of the world, somebody, for a while, will remember the color of our eyes, the tears we shed, the smiles we smiled, and our determination to live. It is good to know that our names will be remembered, because for so long we were just concentration camp numbers: 79212, 79213, 79214.

The number 79215 belongs to Cipi. Cipi, where are you?

We busy ourselves with our belongings. We have bartered away so much that our worldly treasures are light to carry. We help each other. We no longer sell or buy. We give gifts. We give affection.

The train screeches to a halt. Odessa.

We don't know how we will be transported from the railroad station, or where. Inevitably, there will be some chaos with so many people alighting simultaneously from our home in motion.

We quickly hug our friends and anyone else in our farewell path of affection. Chicha, Regina, and I lock hands for fear that in the commotion we might be separated.

'Bye . . . when peace will come, we'll drink to you.

Noisy arrangements, preparations of all kinds, are in progress for our transportation to a rehabilitation center. It is late afternoon, very chilly, April 4, 1945.

The Germans said, *"Mach schnell."* The Russians keep saying, *"Davai, davai,"* or something like it. It seems to mean, "Move quickly." A half-track pulls up. We climb in and are off. The famous Black Sea city of Odessa is bleak, gray, and in rubble. The route we take is in rubble.

The last time we were in a half-track was when we were hauled to Birnbaumel by the Nazis in November 1944. This half-track triggers my memory. We are back in a clearing in a German forest. A host of shivering bones are swaying fragilely in the wintry air. One thousand pitiful creatures, straight from Auschwitz.

Ominous sky. Gray, frozen patch of earth in Nazidom's kingdom. Fat, armed SS men in earnest, momentous conferences. A pile of shovels on the ground.

Yes, we know what all this means. The shovels are to dig our own graves, pits for our bullet-ridden bodies. Did the beasts have to drag us this far for manual killing when the gas chambers and crematoriums were so close at hand at Auschwitz? Or was the murder machinery made inoperative just before we left that dread hell of extermination, or right afterward?

The Germans are the masters of cunning, forever altering their diabolical plans so that we should not be able to outsmart them. As if we could. We were never smart, evil, or devious enough to figure them out. They were smarter and certainly more evil—as when they enticed prisoners, with promises of bread, to voluntarily go on transport. And the following day the duped prisoners' clothing would come back from the crematoriums. Evil is smarter than good.

We weren't murdered in Birnbaumel, but most of the thousand bags of bones perished finally on the snowy death march to Bergen-Belsen.

We promised our friends on the train to try not to remember. Promises are easily broken.

We are on half-tracks again. But now we are garbed in warm clothing, we are not hungry, and our liberators are trying to take care of us. Our lives are not being threatened.

We are in a great city. Why is my memory so stubborn?

We pass the world-renowned opera house. We see a sad-looking city trying to repair its buildings, trying to regain its soul. We see bundled-up children and adults silently welcoming us, the gaping strangers, as we roll by them.

We have been en route for an eternity. We came by foot, by rail, via half-track. Hitler sent us. Thank you for your welcome.

We arrive at the rehabilitation center. The building is enormous, housing an enormous number of displaced people. We are led to a huge room that is filled with sleeping arrangements all over the floor. Languages abound. There are people, people everywhere. There are noises, excitement, expectations. There are new encounters, new friends, new hopes. The same questions.

"Where do you come from?"

"How long were you in Auschwitz?"

"When were you liberated? Where?"

"How many were in your family?"

"How many survived?"

"Where are you going?"

The variety of tales is staggering, as is the number of nationalities present. Not all the people are Jews. Not all are liberated soldiers. Not all are liberated slave laborers.

They are people from everywhere, human beings left over from Hitler's devastating rampage across the continents. The atmosphere is exciting, confusing, and life-affirming, with death and tragedy lurking everywhere in the background.

Chicha has a fever. A Russian doctor attends to her right away.

"Don't be frightened. It's just a bad cold," he comforts in Yiddish. "She'll be well soon. Where are you from?"

"Hungary. We were in Auschwitz. We're Jews."

"I'm a Jew, too. I live here in Odessa. Are you going back to Hungary?"

"Never. We want to go to America."

"I have a brother in America. Will you take a letter to him?"

The doctor is overworked. The Jewish survivors flock to him. They have heard he is Jewish. They are eager to seek solace from a real doctor, a Jewish doctor, one who heals—not a killing doctor, like Dr. Mengele, the Nazi vulture of death.

We tell the Russian healer about Dr. Mengele. He already knows about him. He is in pain.

"Are you sure he is a physician?"

"Yes, we are absolutely certain. Mengele is a physician."

We try to go outside the center. The place is guarded. We are allowed to stand in front of the building for only a few minutes.

I wonder how many Nazis are in the building posing as survivors. I force the thought out of my mind. It is too painful. I cannot deal with it. It is too diabolical. I must stop thinking of anything but America.

THE REHAB CENTER

IT IS STILL April 4, 1945. We spend the rest of the day and night searching, querying. We want answers to all our questions. We want to meet everyone, to find out about life, about death, to discover who has plans for the future, who hasn't. Almost everyone wants to go home.

Don't the death-camp survivors know that there is no one at home?

They refuse to accept the fact. It is worth going home on the slimmest chance that someone, someone, just might be alive. Without hope it is not worth being anywhere.

In our wanderings through the rehab center, we meet a liberated prisoner of war—slight, short, Yiddish-speaking—a uniformed officer from the Royal Air Force. We tell him who we are, where we come from, that our father is in America. We tell him that, unlike all the others who want to go home, we want to go to America. We tell him that if Cipi and Philip, our oldest sister and only brother, are alive anywhere, we are absolutely certain that they, too, will want to go to America. But we don't know what to do about it. The official routine seems to be to send the refugees back to their countries of origin.

The British officer understands everything. He leaves us and returns with instructions: "Meet me here tomorrow morning at 9 A.M. We have an appointment with the American military attaché. I will be your translator. I will help you in every way I can."

The attaché is handsome, intelligent, in control. Each of his questions is translated into Yiddish by the British flier, who is as concerned, as loyal, as if he were a lifelong friend. Having grown up as a Jew in fascist Hungary, I cannot remember a time when we were not afraid of an official. Now these two kind men are able to peel away that ingrained fear. We don't understand how men in uniform, so highly placed, can be so human.

Our whole horrendous experience unfolds in our answers to the questions, which keep coming at us. Each answer saddens the faces of the two men. The interview is long, and the longer it lasts, the closer the five of us feel to one another. We feel comfortable with our new British and American friends. We feel their compassion. We are all very civilized and very sad.

"There will be a ship leaving for America in sixteen days," the American attaché finally says. "You will be on that ship."

Our appointment is over.

Beaming, our British friend guides us back to our quarters. I don't remember seeing him again. I don't remember his name. I will never forget him.

Regina, Chicha, and I hug each other with love and laughter. We are crazily happy. Incredulous. We are going to America. Can such good fortune happen to us with so much grace and speed?

We become instant celebrities—"the three Americans." We have status, happiness, and security. Three homeless, wandering, persecuted Jews have been invited to the New World!

We didn't have to beg. We were accepted. The good man said we would be on that ship. We run through the corridors of the refugee center, kissing Europeans.

"Did you hear? We are Americans! We are Americans!"

Sixteen days. Is that time enough for us to begin to believe there is a country that really wants us to live on its soil? Can we come to terms in such a short period with happiness, unused to joy as we are? Is it time enough for us to say good-bye to a continent that shaped and ruined our lives?

Everything within us is dancing to a lilting song: *You are not despised. You are accepted. You are welcome.*

The song we sing in return is: *Thank you, America. Thank you.*

We sing our way back to our communal bedroom. We are joyfully exhausted. Chicha is still feverish. We lie down to daydream, to relive each moment of this momentous day.

Suddenly, there is a knock on the door. It is the American military attaché, accompanied by two American soldiers carrying three army duffel bags. One of the soldiers speaks broken Yiddish and translates.

"You are leaving for the United States on the SS *Brand Whitlock* tomorrow at 8 A.M.," the attaché informs us. "We've run out of female uniforms, but I've brought along our smallest-size male uniforms. I hope they fit you."

Three army uniforms, caps and all, appear from the duffel bags.

"I'm really sorry," the attaché continues, "but Liberty ships cannot have civilians aboard, so you'll have to dress like WACs. I'll be here in the morning to take you to the pier."

Just as suddenly as he appeared, the attaché departs, leaving the two soldiers behind to help us pack our belongings.

We are in total shock, verging on hysteria. But the shock does not last long. We begin to examine our "wardrobe," acting like American millionaires. We sort our treasures and give gifts to some of the girls we are leaving behind. In the face of our great good fortune, our restraint is minimal.

Our joyful mood lasts half the night. Parting from the others in the morning will be less painful than it was aboard the train, when our future was so fragile. We are now more self-assured, less tearful, less vulnerable. For the first time in our short lives, we go to sleep feeling like Americans.

APRIL 6, 1945

DRESSED IN KHAKI, we are on our way to the pier in an American jeep driven by the American military attaché. On the road I try to piece together the course of events that led up to this moment. I am unable to do so; things have moved so swiftly in the last forty-eight hours. Later, however, I learn what may have happened.

Apparently, the American military attaché was so moved by our story that he contacted his superiors in Washington to ascertain whether our father was indeed living in the United States. Our story proved to be accurate, and the attaché was instructed to place us aboard the first vessel bound for America.

The SS *Brand Whitlock,* which had unloaded a cargo of tanks for the Russians, was leaving the next morning, and the attaché quickly arranged for our passage, together with sixteen liberated American soldiers and a German-American woman who was returning to the States from her fatherland. The woman had been a Nazi sympathizer, although a naturalized U.S. citizen. When Hitler was riding high, she had gone back to Germany to partake in the glory, but now that her erstwhile hero was losing the war, she was scurrying back to her American haven.

At dockside Regina, Chicha, and I, trim in our new military uniforms, alight from the jeep. It can probably not be disputed that we look very attractive. While the attaché boards the ship for last-minute arrangements, the American crewmen on deck, beholding us below, can barely control their delight.

Each face welcomes us. Each wears a smile. We, once despised Jewish girls, are suddenly a delicious sight. We are not abused, lice-filled vermin. Life seems unreal.

It must be real, however, for we feel both the joy of *now* in every vein, and the pain of *then*. Bless you, dear strangers, as you gaze down upon us with affection and curiosity, as we stand in awesome anticipation, as we look up with hope.

The attaché returns and accompanies us to our new home, a floating heavenly home, that will sail on and on and on . . . to America. The attaché introduces us to the various officers and to the captain, who escorts us to a cabin that has been arranged for us.

"Have a pleasant trip," we hear the attaché saying as he shakes hands with us. Then we see him running down the gangplank.

I want to run after him, to hug and kiss him. I want to send a message with him to Hitler, wherever he sits on his disintegrating throne of disaster: "Sir, just one more thing, please. Please tell Adolf that my sisters and I are on the SS *Brand Whitlock,* sailing to America. And, dear sir, we thank you. We thank you ever so much."

I don't move, however, and I never see that good American man again. Oh, my God, what was his name?

Dr. Mengele, we are on our way to America, and we are going to forget every brutal German word you forced us to learn. We are going to learn a new language. We are going to ask for bread and milk in Shakespeare's tongue. We will learn how to live speaking English and forget how people die speaking German.

The ship detaches itself from land and plunges into the waves of the Black Sea. "Good-bye, Dr. Mengele, you murderer. You robbed us of our family. Seven of us were supposed to go to America. Only three of us are leaving."

I search the sky to see if I can conjure up my mother and my little sister, Potyo. I look in desperate sorrow but can discern no human form. The smoke has vanished. There is not a trace. No grave. Nothing. Absolutely nothing.

My mother lived for just a while—Potyo for less than fourteen years. In a way they didn't really die. They simply became smoke.

How does one bury smoke?

How does one place headstones in the sky?

How does one bring flowers to the clouds?

Mother, Potyo . . . I am trying to say good-bye to you. I am trying to say good-bye.

Will Cipi and Philip ever sail the seas?

The captain seats the German-American woman and me at his table, Regina at the next table. Jack, an officer and the only American Jew aboard, instructs the steward to seat Chicha at his table. Later, when we get to know him better, Jack tells us why.

"While you were standing on the pier," he tells us, "I sized you up from the deck.

"This one's cute," he says, pointing to Regina.

"That one's beautiful," he continues.

"But she's the one for me," he concludes, smiling at Chicha.

The captain, sensing my discomfort because of the German woman's presence, is solicitous and kind. He anticipates my needs and pays special attention to me. Still, for reasons I do not understand, I discover that the captain is disliked by the ship's officers and is unpopular with the crew.

Who is the finest, most adored man aboard?

The chief engineer.

The chief engineer's cabin becomes our daily social hall. Each afternoon, Regina, Chicha, and I, together with the off-duty officers, gather there for a jolly time.

How do we communicate?

With gestures, with laughter. Some speak a little German, as we do. Jack translates in Yiddish. And everyone teaches us English.

In return we teach Hungarian, and, in fun, indulge in childish pranks.

I'm sorry, fellows, but *Sarokrád* is not really shredded sour cabbage. *Sarokrád,* in Hungarian, means, "I shit on you."

We never meant it literally, fellows. You know that. It was all in fun. You taught us words, and we taught you words. And we laughed and laughed and laughed.

We have such good times in the chief engineer's cabin. The only one not included is the captain, who, if he knows of our frolics, must be jealous—and, of course, the German woman. No one sees her, other than at eating times. After each meal she disappears below deck, where the crew and the sixteen passenger soldiers are quartered.

We are protected and looked after by everyone on the

officers' deck. The officers are brothers, fathers, teachers to us. They are not lovers, although they do love us. There is only one true love story in the making—Jack and Chicha—and even Chicha herself cannot believe what is happening.

JACK AND CHICHA

IF THE CHIEF ENGINEER'S CABIN is our gathering place for fun and laughter, Jack's cabin is our refuge for tears and comfort. After all, Jack is the only Jew besides us on board, and we have only recently come from a poisonous, Jew-hating world.

We were uprooted from our land of birth, banished, and butchered. We grew up in a country where nearly everyone who was not Jewish disliked or hated almost everyone who was.

Why—because our people pray in a temple that bears no cross?

At home we did have a number of friends who were Christian. Still, they were so few, we could never feel absolutely safe.

On the SS *Brand Whitlock* we love all these good Christian men around us. We truly love them; they are so kind to us. But can they understand our suffering the way Jack, the son and grandson of Jews who had suffered the pogroms of czarist Russia, can understand it? It is too soon for us not to be wary of Christians. It is natural for us to fear gentiles and to turn more readily to a Jew for solace.

Daily, before each meal, Jack, with menu in hand, appears at our cabin. In Yiddish he explains each dish to us, so that we can later point out our choices to the waiter. It is one of Jack's most thoughtful acts, and we are so grateful.

But everything Jack does is thoughtful, from providing aspirin to listening to our sorrow. We are his family; he is ours. We have come from such horror—and have met Jack so near in time to that horror—that our relationship is being forged in a very special way.

Jack is not a survivor. He is a native American, our first Jew from the "good life"; for right now he and the ship are all the good that life can offer.

Jack is modest and somewhat shy. Sharing our sorrow and tales of hardship, he tells us of the Great Depression in America and of the hard times his family has endured, with his father barely eking out a living for his wife and eight children, sometimes earning just enough for potatoes. Now his father is in some kind of trucking business and the family is managing.

Because Jack is the first person from the New World, from across the cleansing sea, to touch our lives intimately, he will always be dear to us in our life ahead. Right now, however, he is especially dear to Chicha.

How do the mysterious forces of love work? Has anyone ever found the answer?

Attraction. Chemistry. Animal magnetism. Love at first sight. Words and clichés explain nothing. Language is feeble when confronted with reality, and the reality aboard this American liberty ship at this moment is that two young strangers, each from a world entirely alien to the other, have met and have been drawn together powerfully and tenderly.

Only twenty-four hours after their first meeting at the dining room table, where Jack ordered Chicha's food for her, the two were openly seeking each other out, finding ways to saunter off together, to be together in odd corners of the vessel at odd hours of the day, to be together beneath the star-filled sky at night.

Up until now, Regina, Chicha, and I have been a virtually inseparable trio; suddenly, Regina and I are finding ourselves increasingly alone, wondering about the whereabouts of our sister Chicha, marveling at the exquisite miracle of it all. Later, when Chicha finally appears, she is radiant and bubbly. She cannot explain exactly where she has been or what is happening to her. Like a mechanical doll, she keeps repeating, "I'm in love. I'm in love. I'm in love."

We are told we can write to my father, telling him that we will see him soon. We don't know how our letter will reach him from the high seas, but we are happy that we can let him know we are on our way. The secrecy shrouding wartime travel and communication makes us feel like characters in some kind of international drama.

An American officer who speaks to us in German reinforces this feeling. His interest is in the German-American woman who is traveling with us. Is there anything we can tell him about her?

There is nothing we can relate; we don't know the woman. But I do recall unexpectedly coming upon her while she was fussing with her collection of Nazi postage stamps, each bearing the likeness of *der Führer*. There she was, kissing the stamps in adoration.

May she and her beloved *Führer* rot together in purgatory!

THE SHIP has been at sea for several days. For some unknown reason, we are on a southeasterly course toward the Caucasus, rather than a southwesterly one toward the Bosporus. Later we learn that the vessel is to take on a cargo of sisal at Batumi, a Russian port at the eastern end of the Black Sea, before heading west.

Regina and I are now accustomed to seeing the unmasked affection between Jack and Chicha. They make no attempt to hide it. We spot them holding each other lovingly, kissing in the corridors, disappearing entirely for long interludes.

A mixture of feelings invades our souls. We are delighted, worried, curious, envious. Still, we recognize that a strange healing process is at work. God, let the process work its magic around the clock. Let there be renewal. Let our fragmented lives become whole again. Let us arrive in the New World with new bodies, new hair, and new hearts, hearts that beat to the sounds of life and love, not fear.

At Batumi some of the crew are permitted to go ashore while the Russian cargo is being loaded on to the American vessel. To our surprise Jack is one of those descending the rope ladder from the SS *Brand Whitlock*.

Chicha cannot believe her eyes as she watches Jack disappear beyond the immediate dock area. Her new-found security, vested in Jack, suddenly seems to have vanished.

"Where's he going?" she asks Regina and me. "Where's he going?" As though we can provide an answer and reassurance.

"He'll be back soon," we tell her. "He must have some business to attend to."

But we are equally anxious and worried, for Jack represents not only something very personal to Chicha, but also, as our translator, our vital link to everyone else on the ship. In addition, we had, even as youngsters, heard about the unreliability of sailors. They were men who had a girl in every port, or so we were told.

After what seems endless hours of on-deck vigil, watching the loading operations and the activity on the dock, we see the American seamen begin to return. Soon we see Jack. He appears to be in good humor—and a bit tipsy.

As Jack makes his way up the dangling ladder, Chicha begins to seethe. She mumbles choice Hungarian epithets. Her relief at seeing "her man" return is mixed with obvious jealousy.

At last Jack is back on board among his fellow officers, who are engaged in jocular banter. So far, he has not seen us, but as he moves along the deck toward his quarters, he suddenly discovers Chicha in his path.

"Did you enjoy the Russian women?"

Jack, not comprehending a single word, opens his arms and breaks into a broad, toothy grin. "Chicha! I missed you. I should have stayed on board."

In a single enveloping gesture, he embraces her, virtually smothering her in his arms.

The next moment, as the two stand kissing, the American officers break into laughter, hoots, and applause. Regina and I, somewhat embarrassed, make our way back to our cabin.

Did we ever dream that we would become world travelers, see the sun sparkle on slender minarets in Istanbul, hear the bustling sounds of a Turkish port? We have sailed clear across the Black Sea, through the Bosporus strait, and are now plowing through the Sea of Marmara. If only we could go ashore and stroll the way we strolled on the way to Odessa.

But we are not allowed to debark anywhere; only some of the crew can do so. We envy them. We are traveling freely, it seems, but in relative confinement, delicious confinement, still not free to explore strange, wondrous places. Someday, when war will not curtail our movements, we shall return.

Our curiosity is vibrantly alive. We learned about Turkey and the Bosporus and the Dardanelles when we were schoolchildren in Hungary. Now, courtesy of World War II and Adolf Hitler, here we are.

Mealtimes are somewhat formal in the dining room. The captain sets the tone, and he is stiff and pompous. We have relearned our table manners, and it is easy to eat with knife and fork leisurely, the way the English did.

There is enough glorious food on the *Brand Whitlock* to satisfy the vultures of Auschwitz. I am overfed. No one can tell that just a few months ago—in January, as a matter of fact—all of me weighed less than parts of me do now. I am actually getting fat.

It is not natural for me to be fat. I am simply stuffed, like a force-fed goose, and nothing will stop me from eating more, much more. If my face is indeed as beautiful as they say, there is a great spread of it. Let it be. I cannot imagine ever intentionally going on a diet to reduce my weight. More readily can I imagine stealing food rather than saying no to any offer.

Then there is the matter of my pride, as with Sam, the waiter, who dislikes me.

Sam and I are unable to communicate with each other, but each of us is capable of a full-blown emotional reaction—a negative one. Sam waits on the captain's table, and he never fails to subject me to an icy glance when he attends to my needs.

I don't know the source of his resentment, but I return the ice. *I don't like you either, Sam.*

Then, one day, it happens. Not being able to speak English, I point to an item on the menu simply because the spelling is similar to a Hungarian word.

"Do you know what you're ordering?" I hear Sam say with ice in his voice.

I nod, praying that the mysterious item will turn out to be a feast.

"Are you sure this is what you want, all you want?"

Bewildered, perspiring from my insecurity, I hold my ground. "Yes," I say in Hungarian. "I know what I want. *This.* This is exactly what I want."

Sam shrugs and disappears. Moments later he returns and triumphantly places my humiliating choice, with its sour odor, in front of my nose—a heaping dish of steaming sauerkraut!

Sam, I really don't like you, nor sauerkraut. But damn it, Sam, I'm going to eat every last shred!

And I do.

———

Although I'm getting heavier, Regina is not. She is seasick much of the time and cannot retain the food she so craves. Still, the security of the ship—all the love, attention, and care—keeps her spirits high. We are all the happier for the bittersweet humor that gushes out of her in Hungarian, for her Yiddish is far weaker than mine or Chicha's.

Chicha and I translate Regina's Hungarian into Yiddish for Jack, who, in turn, translates it into English for the Americans who understand not a word of Hungarian or Yiddish but laugh even before the translation is complete. The Americans respond to us with joy because they want to see us happy. We are their family from another planet, a gift from a place called Auschwitz.

SKIRMISHES

LATE AT NIGHT the dining room is an informal center for social life and snacks. The German woman never joins us. She doesn't belong. She is in self-appointed exile. Either she must feel very guilty, or she actually is.

The late-night snacks are a particularly warm aspect of our glorious, endless rolling on the sea. The officers come in shirtsleeves. They are relaxed and talkative, and our attempts at spoken English are more brazen and funnier than ever. Our gestures in hand-and-feet language are broad and nonsensical, but we all understand each other. We are a very happy family.

On this occasion, all attention focuses on Jack and Chicha. Accidentally, Chicha spills some water on Jack. Playfully, Jack returns the spill. Deliberately, Chicha retaliates. Swiftly, Jack splashes back. Suddenly, bedlam breaks out.

Chicha and Jack, like two combatants, grab for any water in sight. One hurls water at the other, the other hurls back. Splash for splash. Spill for spill.

In moments each is soaking wet. Tables are being shoved about. Dishes and utensils are rattling. Chairs are toppling. The men are scrambling and shouting. The floor is flooded and slippery.

Jack flees into the kitchen. In an instant he is back, pouring a pitcher of water over Chicha's head.

Chicha races into the kitchen. She returns with another pitcher.

Splash!

Jack is dripping and laughing.

Chicha is soaked and laughing.

Water is everywhere—on the tables, the chairs, the walls, the floor. The dining room is literally awash at sea.

Suddenly, the two warriors are locked in a wet, soggy embrace.

The men, now laughing uncontrollably, are standing around applauding.

Regina and I sink into two wet chairs and go limp with joy.

Word of the water skirmish spreads swiftly through the ship, and soon we learn that the crew's late-night snack privilege has been suspended for breach of discipline.

Jack calls the punishment too severe for what he regards as a minor infraction. "It was only a harmless spat," he tells the captain. "The crew shouldn't be punished for something that is basically my fault."

"Are you in love with all three of them or only one?" the captain asks with undisguised envy over Jack's special relationship with us.

Jack ignores the question and reiterates his own responsibility.

After a day or two, with crew resentment mounting, the captain relents and restores the nighttime snack privilege. Interestingly, none of the crew's anger has been directed at Jack or us—only at the captain. Love, obviously, has emerged triumphant, for the feelings between Jack and Chicha are now more securely locked in place.

Thank you, Captain, for letting us all eat again—both day and night.

The memories of war and hatred are never far below the surface of our troubled minds, waiting to be summoned forth. Now, somewhere in the Mediterranean Sea, they break through to the surface. In the still of night, a shrill alert sounds, triggering fear and apprehension. We hear shouts and the sounds of men running in the corridor outside our cabin.

German subs!

Enemy mines!

Danger!

Following the emergency procedures we have been practicing, we rush to the deck, donning our life jackets on the way. Having been rudely awakened, I am completely disoriented and fear-ridden. Oblivious of everyone around me and terrified of freezing in the ocean, I struggle with the first piece of clothing I have grabbed while running from my cabin—a small pink undergarment.

With no ability to act or think intelligently, I try desperately to pull the tiny slip over my life jacket. The more I struggle, the less successful I am.

Suddenly, I become conscious of laughter, uncontrolled laughter. I stop struggling and look about. The entire crew is on deck, watching me. *I* am the object of their laughter. The alert is over.

As the all-clear sounds, I flee back to my cabin in embarrassment.

———

The SS *Brand Whitlock* is gliding its way to the Algerian port of Oran.

Regina, the talented, mothering baby in our shrunken family, is preparing for the blazing sun of North Africa. She slices up some pajamas from our "thieving" days after liberation and begins to fashion three bathing suits. There is not enough fabric to make large suits, so they turn out to be perhaps the first bikinis in the world.

We are complimented by the men with such words as "cover girls" and "glamour girls," and the names of fashion magazines are mentioned that we never heard of. The captain has three canvas chairs scrubbed bone white; they are placed on the top deck for us, and we begin to bake our bodies under a broiling sky millions of miles, millions of years away from the broiling stench of Auschwitz.

Everything good—food, water, showers, the ability to use a bathroom—everything we have reminds us of everything we did not have just a few short months ago. A few months ago we didn't even have bodies enough to bronze under an African sun. We live by constant comparisons. It is hard enough to live in one world; we are destined to live forever in two.

The captain arranges absolute protective privacy for us. No one is to come near us while we sunbathe. Half naked, we recall our joyful childhood summers in the Carpathian Mountains. Reminiscing and dreaming of happier days, we fall asleep.

Late at night, three Hungarian sun goddesses are lobster red, in need of care and sympathy. Jack and the captain touch our shoulders gently. Jack, in charge of first aid, provides us with a soothing ointment.

We return to the open deck to marvel at Oran, the first fully lighted city we have seen since 1939.

At Oran the ship docks briefly while a crewman is escorted ashore for medical treatment. The man had severed a finger in a machine-shop accident below decks, and there is no surgeon aboard to treat him. Soon thereafter, we are sailing away toward Gibraltar, where we are to rendezvous with a convoy of thirty or forty other ships for the transatlantic voyage to America.

The *Brand Whitlock* makes arrangements for a noontime rendezvous, and Regina, Chicha, and I are told to be on deck. Apparently, we three young women, an extraordinary wartime cargo, are to be displayed to the disbelieving, envious eyes of the convoy.

An army of flirtatious, whistling men greets us as our ship passes into position. The men seem more than willing to swim over and transport us to their ships.

A smug, self-satisfied *Brand Whitlock* sails into the Atlantic.

We are inching our way toward a father who cannot be notified of the date of our arrival. We want to see him, but we also want to stay on the ship forever, for life has never been this good to us.

Some nights are chilly as the convoy plows through the giant waves of the ocean. Regina is again protective and creative. She spreads out on deck the one gray blanket we hauled along, cuts it into sections, and, with needle and thread, spends our social afternoons in the chief engineer's cabin fashioning a hooded marvel of a coat that all three of us share from time to time. Somewhere, someone will have to watch over Regina, for she never stops watching over Chicha and me.

ROOSEVELT'S DEATH

APRIL 12, 1945, on the high seas. We don't understand the words on the radio in the dining room. We see only the gloom around us.

Can there have been a reversal of all our fortunes? Is Hitler winning the war again? Will the world become a morgue? Is history's longest arm of evil reaching us right across the ocean?

The men listen to the radio intently. We dare not interrupt. We are afraid to learn of new catastrophes. A sorrowful cloud hangs over us. There are detectable tears.

"Jack, are there Yiddish words for the trouble?"

"Yes. President Roosevelt is dead."

Suddenly, a painful memory seizes us. Roosevelt was going to be our president, too; but we remember him also as our failed savior.

The last country to be occupied by Nazi troops was Hungary. Everyone was saying that it is up to Roosevelt to save Hungary's Jews. The war is in its final phase. Hitler is no longer as strong as he was. Perhaps now he could be negotiated with for the last remnants of European Jewry.

We don't know what actually happened to the other

Jews. We know only that we are the last ones on Hitler's death list, and the teeth of the beast are not as sharp as they used to be. Maybe there is hope for us—but only if President Roosevelt comes to our aid.

Rumors fly from Hungarian town to Hungarian town. Rumors of ransoms. Rumors of exchanges. Jews for gold. Jews for trucks. All kinds of secret negotiations are said to be taking place, and the possibilities are always connected with the American president.

On March 19, 1944, the Nazi killers finally enter Hungary. But hope is still alive. Every Jewish prayer is tied to Roosevelt. Roosevelt will save us.

Why, then, are we in the cattle cars?

We share the Americans' grief, but there is a separate compartment of Jewish tragedy in our hearts that is linked ambivalently with this American president. We cry over his death and for the millions of Jewish funerals we never had. Our mourning is awash in complexities we cannot untangle. Our pain ducts open and close. With a newfound loyalty to a country we were not born in, but want to be natives of, we mourn along with the Americans.

The SS *Brand Whitlock* keeps chopping the waves of the Atlantic, speeding us to a reacquaintance with our father, speeding us to a land of new culture, new language, new faith in a better tomorrow. Our old luggage keeps weighing us down, imprisoning us with all we carry in our minds. We yearn to rest our cluttered heads on a new continent, separated by great waters from the cursed continent on which we were born.

We have been at sea for more than a month. It is now May 6, and we are drawing closer to the shores of the

United States. Chicha, Regina, and I huddle together in Jack's cabin.

Jack talks to us about this new world we are about to encounter: skyscrapers, buildings that rise to the clouds in New York; the world's tallest building, the Empire State; Times Square and Forty-second Street, the "crossroads of the world," where there is a blaze of lights not from a single movie house, as in Kisvárda, but from an entire block of movie houses.

He tells us about the New York Times Building and its exterior flashing news ribbon that will spell out the word *Peace* in electric lights; about the subway trains that carry millions of people underground, going or returning from places where they earn their livelihood; about trolley cars clanking in a bustling metropolis, where, through the noise, every accent, every language can be heard from every corner of the world.

He speaks of Ellis Island and New York harbor, where millions of immigrants have been greeted by a "Lady" holding high a torch of liberty; of Manhattan Island, where people can be seen wearing native clothes from far off hamlets or designer clothes from Paris, where one can eat Jewish rye bread, Kansas beef, or Chinese delicacies.

He describes a land where the color of people's skin can vary from white to black, from yellow to red; where people can be Protestant, Baptist, Buddhist, or Catholic —even Jewish or atheist—and they all live together in that melting pot called democracy; where people ride in huge automobiles or sweat in the belly of the earth; where there are slums and estates with private tennis courts, tall Texans and short Mexicans, the very rich and the very poor, a great many people who are neither rich nor poor, just citizens of a free country, a country very different from those we have known.

We listen with rapt attention as Jack talks on and on about his country, about the country that is soon to be ours. We are eager to learn, and he "teaches" us more and more, both good and bad. He speaks of justice and injustice, of fairness and decency. He tells us of lynchings and the Ku Klux Klan, of "No Jews Allowed" country clubs and "Whites Only" toilets in the South. But, he assures us, there is also a constant churning for change for the better.

America is a land where hate has an air of impermanence; where women can vote and there are secret ballots; where money clanks louder than anywhere else, because there is so much of it; where even the president can be addressed as "you" or "mister"; where nothing is just right but perhaps less wrong than in almost any other place in the world. America is a land where bad can be, and often is, made better.

"You are going to an imperfect country," Jack says finally, "where your lives can be better than anytime before. There are anti-Semites everywhere; still, you will feel relatively equal."

Before we return to our quarters, Jack kisses each of us and hands us a twenty-dollar bill. "I may not be with you when we arrive," he says. "I may be on duty, but I will get in touch."

We have never seen American currency before; twenty dollars seems like a lot of money. We wonder whether he can afford it.

MY SORROW

THE SHIP was en route for five weeks, and then we arrived. She and I. Like two good friends. No! Not at all. I don't like her, but she likes me. She follows me everywhere, refuses to separate from me, even though I hadn't promised to bring her along. On the contrary. But she came anyway. I pleaded with her. "Look," I said, "it's been enough. Stay behind. You've followed me incessantly, but there's a limit. There is little room. It is crowded here, and you are such a giant." As if I wasn't speaking to her at all, she followed me into my cabin. She was ugly, an intolerable travel companion. I was forever trying to leave her behind.

If she stayed and I arrived alone, everything would be different—a new human being, in a new world, starting a new life. I'll go out on the deck and dump her in the ocean, I thought. Let her swim back where she came from, Europe. Puff, puff, choke to death, drop dead. What do I care? Mission accomplished, I was on my way back to the cabin. Suddenly, a voice within: You thought so, eh? No! No!

I am enduring her again, as I did so often. It is only forty-eight hours more. Only twenty-four. I can already see the land. I am looking forward to the new world. She keeps dragging me back. I am begging her, "Stay behind! There is a new world out there. I want to see it. I want to live. With you it is not possible. *I beg you!*"

She interrupts me. She is cold. Merciless. She tells me what I was afraid she'd say: *"I will live as long as you do."*

When we arrived, not even the people standing next to me noticed the ugly, clumsy giant putting her arms around me.

What is a normal life span?

BOOK THREE
AMERICA

BALTIMORE, MARYLAND

MAY 8, 1945. The SS *Brand Whitlock*, bearing the very first survivors of Auschwitz to the United States, is slipping into the harbor at Newport News, Virginia.

Cipi! Philip! The war is over!
It is VE Day, and Hitler's war is over!
And we are in America!

We are numb. This remarkable coincidence of timing defies our ability to deal with the reality. We cannot believe that we are in the center of modern man's most momentous day. To arrive in America on the very day the war ends is too much for us to demystify. It seems entirely unlikely that any survivors of Auschwitz have preceded us. The importance of this soon becomes apparent: We are informed that we have an 8 A.M. appointment the following morning with some American officials.

May 9, 1945. Regina, Chicha, and I are ushered to a large conference room on the ship by a middle-aged man in a military uniform. The man speaks perfect Hungarian and is one of several important-looking men with briefcases. We discover later that they are from the FBI.

The Hungarian-speaking American asks us gently about Auschwitz. Can we please tell him what we know —in detail?

We tell him about Dr. Mengele, the SS Angel of Death. We tell him about Irma Grese, his beautiful female counterpart.

After Mengele, Grese was the most feared deadly force in our lives. She was the *Oberscharführerin,* seemingly more in charge of our daily existence than anyone else. From the roots of her hair to the nails on her toes, Grese was saturated with deeds so evil and so abhorrent that the likes of her could not ever have been part of the human family.

We are calm and soft-spoken. Our tale in Hungarian sounds even more horrifying than when we tried to tell the same story in Yiddish to the English flier in Odessa. Even from this distance, I feel the terror of the time that Grese let her German shepherd loose on a helpless prisoner.

"If you make a sound," Grese warned us, "you are next."

In silent, sickening horror, we stood by and watched the German attack dog chew up the shrieking human being.

(Soon after the war, Irma Grese was one of the Nazi war criminals to be caught, tried, convicted, and hanged. I wonder whether our testimony on that May 9 was used at her trial, whether we helped in some small way to eliminate the beast.)

The morning wears on. The questions are weighing us down, but we know that the information we are conveying is important, so we summon our strength and supply the answers. Much of our memories we would like to bury at the bottom of the ocean, but some of our answers relate to happier events, such as our liberation.

Finally, the officials pack our lives into their briefcases, bid us farewell, and we rejoin our *Brand Whitlock* family.

Only hours are left of our togetherness. "Good-bye time" is upon us again. Our blessed ship is sailing the last few miles of its healing journey. We are on our way to the last stop of our twentieth-century odyssey.

It is Thursday, May 10, 1945. We anchor at a port on the Patapsco River estuary near Chesapeake Bay. Four and a half weeks and half a world away from Odessa, Regina, Chicha, and I leave the kindest floating haven in the world. We step gingerly onto the soil of the United States and into the American city of Baltimore, Maryland.

We leave tears and thanks with the human beings who were so good to us. Jack will contact us, he assures us in a hasty parting, on his first free day in New York. With the exception of Jack and a chance encounter with one of the ship's officers some years later, we never see any of our mentors again.

It is raining heavily in Baltimore. It is late afternoon as immigration officers guide us to a streetcar. Arrangements have been made with Judge Simon E. Soboloff, one of Baltimore's most distinguished Jewish citizens and the future solicitor general of the United States, to be our host until our father is located.

We step on the streetcar and, for the first time in our lives, see black people. We gape, too innocent even to be embarrassed about our shock and delight. They look so beautifully suntanned, so healthy, that I wonder, almost aloud, whether the white people around us are suffering from consumption. In our ignorance and naïveté, and because the blacks are clustered together in one part of the trolley, we speculate whether they all might be of the same family. We are overwhelmed by the sudden foreignness of everything around us.

We finally reach our destination, a large, beautiful home, and are greeted warmly by Mrs. Sobeloff, a short, blond bundle of loving care. Mrs. Sobeloff, a socially conscious woman, is deeply involved with the National Council for Jewish Women and is more than ready to assume the role of substitute mother to three Hungarian orphans.

Shortly thereafter, Judge Sobeloff arrives with his two friendly daughters. Immediately, instinctively, we know that the Sobeloffs have adopted us for lifelong friendship.

While we dine in unaccustomed elegance, Judge Sobeloff makes an exhausting series of phone calls to find our father in New York. Intermittently, he asks us in Yiddish for bits of information that may aid his search.

There is no M. Katz listed at the address we provide; there is no M. Katz anywhere near that address. Also, there are many Katzes in New York, but none who is our father.

After a great deal of struggle with telephone operators and their supervisors, Judge Sobeloff reaches a resident at the first address we gave him.

"Is there a man named M. Katz living in your building? This is very important."

"I have a neighbor whose brother is living with her. His name is Katz, but I don't know if he's the man you want."

"Would you please be kind enough to get him? His children are looking for him."

After a long interval a voice responds in Hungarian.

I take the receiver and listen. The voice belongs to my aunt, who emigrated to America when I was just a child. I remember vaguely what she looks like but little else. She is talking to me rapidly in her native tongue.

"Yes, we know you're alive. A letter fell out of my daughter's schoolbook telling us you were on your way."

I wonder how the letter got there. It is too mysterious.

"Your father's not here. He's in temple. He's praying. He prays all the time. We'll find him. Give us your number. You'll hear from us soon. Thank God you're alive."

At Simon Sobeloff's home we all sit vigil, waiting. It is late when the phone finally rings. My father is weeping at the other end.

We have no answers to his questions. We are frightened, bewildered. What can we say to him? We recognize his voice but can't believe we have a parent.

We know that he cannot come to us immediately because of the closeness of the Sabbath. We are prepared for what he tells us—immediately after the Sabbath he will board a train and be with us early Sunday morning.

He blesses our hosts and promises to take care of everything when he sees us. He will have papers and will reimburse the government for our passage. He will spend the Sabbath praying for the safe arrival of the rest of his family.

For two days we try not to think about what to tell my father. It is easy and pleasant to be with the Sobeloffs. We do not share family tragedy with them. With my father it will be different.

We are cared for with tenderness and kindness. We keep finding new families but cannot put ours together. The first thing we'll do in New York is place an ad in a paper:

"Has anyone seen Cipi or Philip?"

LYING TO MY FATHER

IN ANTICIPATION of our father's arrival, breakfast is served very early Sunday morning at the Sobeloff home. The sweets taste sour. The sour tastes sweet. The chaos in our emotions affects even our taste buds.

We are afraid of the impending meeting. Whoever the bureaucrats were in Washington throughout the war years, they did not issue the necessary documents to our father with urgent dispatch so that he could save his family before Hitler devoured them. The bureaucrats played the game of red tape, of rules and regulations, up to the last hideous moment.

If the bureaucrats had let our father bring his family to the United States without the hocus-pocus of immigration papers, then Dr. Mengele would have been cheated of the pleasure of sending one more Jewish family to the ovens. In the face of such deadly danger, should not that have been reason enough to bypass the insanity of bureaucratic paper pushing? After all, our father was a legal resident of the United States, having resided in the country for years, and just a bit of time away from full citizenship.

And now our father is going to be here within the hour, and he will ask us, "Where is Mother? Where is

Cipi? Where is Potyo, my youngest child? Where is Philip, my only son, my *Kaddish?*"

"Father, Father," we will say, "they are on their way."

We will lie and lie. We will not tell him the truth. We cannot bear the truth. We hate ourselves. We hate the whole world.

We are standing in the Sobeloff living room, hugging, weeping, and lying to an aging man. We have found a father, and it is inherent in the larger tragedy that we have also lost him.

There is a profound, instant aura of alienation between us. There are long moments of silence. Our father was in agony for years, but he was in agony in America. We were in agony in Auschwitz.

The gap is too wide. How can we transmit the scent, the smoke, the pall of Auschwitz? The countless dead will all narrow down to two charred bodies, Mother and Potyo. Our father will not be able to accept this kind of truth, and we will not force it down his wounded throat.

The Sobeloff living room is awash with all that Hitler wrought.

GOD?

FOR ALL HIS YEARS, my father kept his faith with the Almighty in the heavens. If the entrance to the heavens is the sky, the sky has been brutalized. It lost its color of blue when Dr. Mengele painted it weeping gray. The fire leaping toward the heavens was kept aglow with the bodies of our mothers, our children.

What is my father to do with his servitude to God? Take Him to task? Perhaps, my father says, we have all been punished for sinning against the Almighty.

My father turns more fanatically religious than ever.

We are now living in a spacious apartment, after a brief sojourn at my aunt's house. At first my father tiptoes around us with pleas for godliness, then he grows more demanding. He wants us to live a life of total devotion. He tries to literally bribe us into believing in the mercy of God.

All we want to do is live, Father. We cannot solve your quarrel with your God. Our brains are too worn for the battle, Father. Let us be.

Newspaper, radio, and film people seek us out. They want to interview us, the first Auschwitz survivors in America, to see if we are real.

My father bars the door to all of them. We are grateful

for that. Then, in earnest, people from all over the country begin to flock to our house.

"Have you seen my mother? Her name was Sarah."

"Have you seen my father, my sisters?"

"We come from Munkács . . . from Beregszaz . . . from Nyíregyháza. Have you seen my brother? What happened to my family? When do you think they'll be coming? How lucky you are to be the first to come."

What do these people want from us? Don't they know what happened?

They are all beggars. They want us to give them something that no longer exists—their families. They want us to give them their Sarahs and Yankeles and Rivkalas, and they are no more. They are practically forcing us to give them a crumb of hope.

But we are not in the business of providing impossible hope. The hope we have, we need to live on. We cannot squander it on lies.

Ask Dr. Mengele. He knows. He must be living somewhere in luxury. He was the Almighty in Auschwitz. He had the power over the lives of all these people you are asking us to remember.

We remember no one. There is no one.

The door bell rings. There is a uniformed man at the door. It is Jack.

"Father, this is the good man we spoke to you about. This is the man who was thoughtful enough to give us money when we disembarked from the *Brand Whitlock*.

"Father, he was so good to us. His name is Jack, and we owe him twenty dollars."

"I am grateful to the officer and will return his money. But not today. Today is the Sabbath, and we do not handle money on the Sabbath."

Silly Jack! How could you? We told you about our father. We told you how religious he was. Couldn't you have come tomorrow?

Poor Chicha is aching to embrace and kiss her love, but she must pretend that he is merely a friend. We must all pretend.

Jack will never do for my father. He is not religious; he is practically a goy, a gentile. He rang the door bell on the Sabbath. He probably came by taxi on the Sabbath.

Jack doesn't want to leave. He just sits there, in love, silent, bewildered, afraid to step on anyone's holy toes.

We all sit there. We all look dumb. Everyone is uncomfortable.

The officer has been sitting there too long. What does he want?

There is no suspicion yet, but a germ of it is growing.

Finally, Jack slips a telephone number to Chicha and leaves.

Everything is Hitler's fault. Everything is due to the war. If my mother were alive, she would smooth things, as she always did. She would negotiate my father's unreasonable demands.

My father hugs me. He pleads with me to go to temple.

"Go upstairs where the women are. Pray for your mother. Pray for the dead."

But the dead didn't just die, Father. They were murdered! I am not grateful for that, Father. My lips freeze in temple. I cannot praise the Lord. I am trying so hard to live with the clutter in my head. Let me be.

Live the way you can, Father. Let me live the way I can. Please.

PHILIP IS ALIVE

A LETTER HAS ARRIVED from an American soldier, Private First Class Berent: "We liberated your son. He is in a hospital. He tried to escape and the Nazis shot him. He is not seriously injured. He is fine. He'll be perfectly all right."

Should I go to temple?

My father is there now.

It will take several months before Philip can be with us, but we can make peace with the waiting period. All we wanted to know was that he was alive, in good enough condition to repair whatever damage he sustained.

Philip, do you know anything about Cipi?

We place an ad in the Hungarian-language newspaper begging anyone with knowledge of Cipi to get in touch with us.

No one responds.

We cry in Hitler's wilderness.

My father writes to Private First Class Berent:

If it isn't asking too much, could you please write another brief letter concerning the whereabouts of my son. Is he still in the hospital?

I have sent letters to my friends in Switzerland, England, and France, instructing them to care for my son, if possible. I will bring him to New York from any one of those countries.

Also, please tell my son to pursue his religion as befits a Jewish boy like him. Please aid my son in any way. I will reimburse you immediately for any expenses.

Enclosed is a money order for my son, Philip.

Sending you and my son my everlasting love, I remain yours, M. Katz.

P.S. If possible, please ask my son to write a letter in his own handwriting.

Philip's survival strengthens and reaffirms my father's faith. Regina, Chicha, and I are deeply religious in our love for our brother—and for our father—but we cannot come to terms with the countless dead.

My father suffers. He cannot compromise the way he lives. And we suffer. We are not asking him to abandon his faith. We just cannot live his way. Our minds are hardly clear about anything. We know only that the mountain in front of our vision is too mammoth.

My father's questions about my mother's arrival become less frequent. We wonder how much he knows. We never spell out details, to him or anyone. The "ugly thing" sits inside us, sealed, as in an iron box.

We had to speak about it in Odessa and on the ship, but from here on, we may not be able to talk about it for decades, perhaps ever.

From here on, we shall just try to live.

JULIET OF AUSCHWITZ

CHICHA uses a public telephone to call Jack at the number he gave her. She tells him that we have a live brother. Jack loves the news. He loves Chicha. They agree to meet secretly on a street corner, Delancey and Essex.

They meet the next day, and the next, and the next. No one sees them until an uncle accidentally encounters them on the subway. The uncle rushes to inform my father, whose suspicion is now confirmed—the goy in uniform is more than a friend.

My father is in a quandary. Till now, all his dreams and plans for his family have been shattered. First by Hitler and his henchmen, then by Roosevelt and his bureaucrats. Through it all, however, he has maintained his faith in his God.

He has prayed and practiced his religion with pious devotion. He has not questioned the nature or the will of the Almighty. He has sacrificed and mourned in his fashion. Throughout the years of separation from his family, he has lived on a Spartan diet, forgoing his favorite foods as a symbolic identification with his hungry and oppressed people. His handsome, tailored suits he hung in the darkest recesses of his closet, where they remained

unworn, growing stale with disuse, a self-imposed depri-
vation.

And God, in His mysterious manner, had blessed him
by returning three daughters to his hearth and by saving
his only son, who ultimately would say *Kaddish,* the
holy prayer for the dead, when in good time the Lord
would call his son's aged father to His fold.

Now, once again, ungodly forces and man-made cir-
cumstances were conspiring to threaten the proper and
holy order of his destiny. His daughter Chicha was in
imminent danger. A stranger, an alien, beardless, nonde-
votional "Jew" was luring his child away from her heri-
tage.

*What could he do to separate and keep this goy, this
Jack, from his divinely returned daughter, the direct de-
scendant of holy rabbis?*

At first he cajoles, pleads, and reasons. He invokes the
name of God, the blessings of God, the wrath of God.
Calamity upon calamity has befallen those who have de-
parted from the paths of righteousness, the way of the
Book, the customs of their people. A Jewish maiden
must pursue the sacred path of her forebears. She must
seek a mate in accordance with divine dictates and with
paternal approval. She must honor and respect the will
of her father.

But an abyss, neither of my father's making nor of
ours, has opened between us. A force that is ungoverned
by reason, by logic, by ancestral practice has taken control of the souls of the participants in this Hitler-created
drama.

Chicha and Jack, who can communicate verbally with
each other only through an elementary command of the
Yiddish language, have nevertheless been drawn together through a silent, voiceless communication that

transcends such barriers as mere words. This type of communication recognizes no abysses, no gulfs, no dictums. It bridges them all, and Chicha and Jack are determined to cross that bridge together. My father must recognize that this, too, is the will of God.

I am taken to visit the second of my three aunts, my father's sisters, who also live in New York. I am not averse to staying with this aunt for several days. She is kind and warmhearted. But I begin to miss my sisters. I cannot understand why they don't call me.

I call the neighbor with the telephone at my father's address and leave word for my sisters to contact me. They don't. I hear not a word from them. What is going on?

I begin to feel insecure. I feel isolated and deserted. I call again. They still do not respond. The enigma is tearing me apart.

I don't know my way around this huge metropolis called New York. I don't know anything about subways. My aunt's phone is silent. I can no longer endure my anxiety.

I pack my bags, kiss my aunt, and run for a taxi. I hand the driver the slip of paper with my father's address and listen to the racing of my heart.

When the taxi arrives, I run to the room my sisters and I have been sharing. Regina and Chicha are in bed, undressed.

"We couldn't call you because they took away our clothes."

Chicha is fuming. "They don't want me to see Jack," she says, "but soon I'm going to meet him like this."

"I gave them my clothes, too," says Regina. " 'If

Chicha can't go out,' I told them, 'I don't want to go out, either.' "

"Here, put these on." I hand them some clothes from my bag, and they dress swiftly. Moments later the three of us are on our way to the aunt I just left. This aunt, at least, is sympathetic to our plight.

At a public phone, Chicha calls Jack and arranges to meet him just once more—to say good-bye. Everything has become much too difficult.

Jack gives her a relative's address, and we place her in a cab. We inform my aunt that Chicha has gone to tell Jack that she can never see him again.

Later, Chicha calls to say that Jack's relative has invited her to stay overnight. It is very difficult to separate forever. We simply must understand. We do.

The following day, Jack, Chicha, and Jack's youngest brother spend the hours in urgent activity. Jack is still in service; therefore, he can get a premarital blood test right away. He does, and the three "conspirators" hurry to the Lower East Side, a predominantly Jewish neighborhood, to find a rabbi holy enough to satisfy even my fanatically religious father.

They find just such a rabbi but then discover that they also need a *minyan*, ten Jewish men, to be present during the sacred rites of a Jewish ceremony. The *minyan* is not an absolute necessity, but having one will add an extra measure of orthodoxy to the marriage.

Jack and his brother race down the street and, at random, round up ten religious-looking Jews. They have their *minyan*.

Jack has purchased a wedding band. Chicha is wearing a borrowed dress. The *minyan* is standing by. And the rabbi performs the ceremony.

The day is June 7, 1945, exactly thirty days after our arrival in the United States.

In Brookline, Massachusetts, Jack introduces his bride to his parents and the other members of his family.

Chicha is dumbfounded.

Jack, the merchant seaman she married, is not a poor American at all. He is, in fact, the son of a very wealthy man!

May you live in peace forever, Romeo of the Seas, Juliet of Auschwitz.

MIRROR

THEY ARE MARCHING to the smell of death. Their
boots are shining like mirrors reflecting the smoke that
fills the earth, the heavens.

It is a year later, and my aunt pleads with me to put
on some lipstick so that I might look like an American,
and I refuse because I don't know yet how people live, I
know only how they die—not how they die in real life, in
normal life, only how they are murdered by the millions
—I am all confused. I come from another planet, or my
aunt does.

Then I accept the little mirror handed to me, and the
lipstick. And I make believe that I am here, alive, like
other people. Yes, I will make my lips beautiful, red, vi-
brant. I will look like other people, and nobody will
know where I come from. If I look like everyone else,
most assuredly I will feel like everyone else. I will have
conquered it all.

My hands are not steady, but now I am determined. I
begin to move the lipstick on my upper lip, and I look
into the mirror. But all I can see is smoke . . . smoke
circling madly on the mirror. I can't see what I am doing.
My lips are red, huge, smeared. I am wearing the grin of
a clown.

And my aunt weeps softly.

MAY

MAY IS SUCH a "big" month. The first of May has overtones of political celebrations, and that is meaningful to me. In my teens, the first of May meant serenading under your window, a burst of spring, love, music, all sentimentally shouting hosannas in your body, masking the dread of reality.

May 1 is my sister's birthday. There is something special about being born on May 1, and dear little Regina is special. There is something special about being born any time in May—May 1, May 28. The scent of spring is delicious. It permeates the air. It sings the song of birth, of life. All is drenched in sun. The earth smiles. It is happy you are here.

The world ended in May. I was born in May. I died in May. We started the journey of ugliness on May 29. We headed for Auschwitz. We arrived on May 31.

The scent of spring wasn't delicious. The earth didn't smile. It shrieked in pain. The air was filled with the stench of death. Unnatural death. The smoke was thick. The sun couldn't crack through. The scent was the smell of burning flesh. The burning flesh was your mother.

I am condemned to walk the earth for all my days with the stench of burning flesh in my nostrils. My nostrils are damned. May is damned. May should be abolished. May hurts. There should be only eleven months in a year. May should be set aside for tears. For six million years, to cleanse the earth.

For more than twenty years I have walked zombielike toward the end of May, deeply depressed, losing jobs, losing lovers, uncomprehending. And then June would come, and there would be new zeal, new life.

Now I am older, and I don't remember all the pain, and June hurts, and so does May. May laughs sometimes, and so does June, and now in May I bend down to smell the flowers, and for moments I don't recall the smell of burning flesh. That is not happiness, only relief, and relief is blessed. Now I want to reinstate the month of May. I want to reincarnate the month, reincarnate the dead. I want to tell my mother that I kept her faith, that I lived because she wanted me to, that the strength she imbued me with is not for sale, that the god in man is worth living for, and I will make sure that I hand that down to those who come after me.

I will tell them to make what is good in all of us their religion, as it was yours, Mother, and then you will always be alive and the housepainter will always be dead. And children someday will plant flowers in Auschwitz, where the sun couldn't crack through the smoke of burning flesh. Mother, I will keep you alive.

1959—PETER

MAMA, MAMA, I'm pregnant!

Isn't that a miracle, Mama? Isn't it incredible, Mama?

I stood in front of the crematorium, and now there is another heart beating within that very body that was condemned to ashes. Two lives in one, Mama—I'm pregnant!

Mama, we've named him Peter. You know how much I like that name. It translates into stone, or rock. You were the rock, Mama. You laid the foundation. Peter has started the birth of the new six million.

Mama, you did not die!

Mama, he weighed seven pounds, four and a half ounces. I weighed only seven times that much when the housepainter painted thick, gray streaks in the sky.

And when I gently ease the bottle between his tender lips and he is satisfied, drinking life, I too am drunk with life. But I cannot help it, Mama, I remember.

I remember the two longest nine months of my life— the nine months while I was counting the seconds to see the life within me, and the nine months while I was dazed, half-crazed, wondering whether the liberators would come in time to save a single heartbeat.

It is all crazy, Mama. Life is ebbing away in the mad pictures of my mind. Life is being nourished in my arms. Help me, Mama. Help me to see only life. Don't let me see the madman anymore.

1961—RICHARD

MAMA, MAMA, the shadow of the madman is fading!
We have another son, Mama. We have named him
Richard. He is like nothing else on the face of the earth.
He looks like Uncle Joe and Aunt Sara, like all of our
cousins, like all of our family.

He looks like nobody else.

He is the sound of your soul. He is the voice of the six
million. He is Richard.

CIPI . . . CIPI . . .

YEARS HAVE PASSED. Each of us is married. And we all have brought forth new life—beautiful, intelligent children.

I *know* that Cipi is dead. Still, I never stop looking.

The lady serving me in the bakery strongly resembles someone I knew. *It cannot be Cipi.* But would it hurt to ask whether she is Hungarian?

On the street, I pursue a lady whose walk resembles Cipi's. I follow her for a couple of blocks, futilely.

It is crazy, but decades later, a few survivors of the Holocaust, I hear, have met kin who were believed to have been murdered by the Nazis. I don't know such cases, but I am told that such miracles have happened. So I look. I always look.

Then something happens.

In 1978, a friend invites me to a gathering of Hungarian survivors. I rarely go to such events, but this time I do.

"Where are you from?" a stranger inquires.

"Kisvárda," I respond.

"Next door to my wife's hometown."

"What's her name?"

"Eva . . . Eva Fülöp." And he presents his wife to me.

"Oh, my God! Eva! Eva! Eva!"

We hug and kiss and weep. We cannot stop. The last time we saw each other was on the infamous winter death march in Germany, January 23, 1945, the day Chicha, Regina, and I escaped, the day we lost Cipi.

Eva is one of six beautiful sisters who suffered with us in Auschwitz and Birnbaumel. We were inseparable; we had to be. During *Zählappell, Wurstappell,* whatever *Appell,* all the prisoners had to line up in rows of five; and to be in a row of five was always the responsibility of the individual prisoners.

Whenever five prisoners got together, it was with the hope that they would form a lasting quintet. Almost always, the hope was thwarted. Some prisoners were taken on work transport; some went to the crematorium; some simply died and disappeared.

To secure a row of five was a never-ending struggle. Only Eva's family and my family were relatively secure. My family of four sisters were short one prisoner for the required five; Eva's family of six had one too many. Together we constituted two rows of five. We couldn't let each other out of sight. Our relationship was full of love, dissonance, and absolute dependence on one another. Miraculously, Eva and all her sisters survived.

"Eva, tell me what happened to Cipi. You know. So please tell me."

Eva begins the story. And I begin to weep. I cry such bitter tears that Eva stops. She refuses to say another word.

In 1980, two years later, I am ready to hear the tale. On a quiet Sunday afternoon, sitting in my secure kitchen, I steel myself and call Eva.

"Listen carefully, Eva. You are not facing me now. You cannot see me. Please tell me exactly what happened to Cipi. I promise not to cry."

"All right. I will tell you. . . .

"After you and Chicha and Regina ran from the column, Cipi started after you. But it was too late. You three got away, but the SS caught Cipi.

"They dragged her back to the column and began to beat her with their rifle butts. They beat and beat and beat her.

"We, too, planned to escape, but when we saw what they did to Cipi, we decided to wait. We weren't brave. We just marched on with the column.

"Cipi was in tragic shape, so we adopted her. We shielded her as if she were our sister. We told her to do whatever we did, to be one of us. We pleaded with her, begged her to try to escape with us.

"But she was in a deep depression. She rejected all our efforts to save her. She shook her head or was totally unresponsive.

"She kept begging the SS to shoot her, but because this was what she wanted, they refused. They knew that her sisters had escaped, and her suffering could be greater by keeping her alive.

"You know how it was. You couldn't die when you wanted to die—only when the SS wanted you dead.

"Finally, we escaped. But Cipi remained on the march. She was too weak and too frightened to try again. We found out later from someone that she actually reached Bergen-Belsen, where she was liberated by the British.

"Then she died."

PHILIP HAD NEVER TALKED about his experiences after he was taken as a slave laborer by the SS from Auschwitz. The most he ever said was that he had been in six concentration camps—and he had survived.

Then, one wintry day, during a wide-ranging conversation in his home, he suddenly began to talk about his final days as a prisoner of the Nazis. In essence, this is what he said:

The Nazis were in full retreat on all fronts. The Russians were closing in from the east, and the Allies were advancing from the west. But the Germans were still fighting, and though they were losing, they were determined to kill as many Jews as possible before they surrendered.

To fulfill this murderous objective, they were transporting about four thousand of us, in their usual cattle cars, to some unknown killing ground.

I probably weighed no more than a child at the time and had no more than a few hours of life left in me. I was very ill and very weak. But I made one last desperate effort to survive.

We had not eaten for days. There was no food on the train, not even for the Nazis. And every few miles, the train was forced to stop because of bombing from the air.

Each time the bombs fell, we had to leave the cattle cars and lie down on the ground a short distance from the train. And each time this happened, a few SS, and one or two civilian trainmen, would desert and disappear into the woods. This told us that our liberators must be very close at hand.

With some trepidation, a Czech prisoner and I decide to gamble on a deal with the SS man in charge of us. We know we cannot trust him—he can kill us just for speaking to him—but we also know that he must be scared because the Allies are so close. If we can gain some time—an hour or two—perhaps we can be liberated by the Allied troops, whose guns we can hear in the distance.

Suppressing our fear, we approach the SS. "If you don't move us," we tell him, "we will tell the Americans that you treated us well when they get here."

The SS is taken aback by our audacity, but he doesn't shoot us. "My duty is to take you to your destination," he says.

"But it's all over. You can hear the American guns. You can save us, and we can save you."

"I don't need your saving." He raises his gun. "Now you'd better be quiet."

Sensing his lack of assurance, we abandon all caution. "The Americans will kill you, or we will kill you," we threaten. It is an incredibly laughable situation—two emaciated skeletons threatening an armed, but frightened, SS man. Finally, as the rumble of guns grows louder, we reach a tacit agreement. The SS will not force us back on the train, and we will do what we can for him.

Suddenly, the SS man says, "You know I wouldn't kill you. Don't you?" He begins to look intimidated and scared. His arrogance, which till now masked his underlying cowardice, is totally gone.

Still, I cannot trust what he says. The Germans, in the past, have been too deceitful. After all his promises, the SS man could easily turn and mow us down. So I ask permission to go to the woods to urinate, hoping to get as far from him as possible.

Just inside the woods, I find another SS deserter hastily changing his uniform for civilian attire.

Startled by my catching him in the act, he deliberately shoots me in the leg. Moments later, the cattle cars are captured by the Allies.

Amid the wild sounds of liberation, and before I fall unconscious, I see a group of female prisoners pounce on their SS guard. They trample, kick, bite, and tear her apart.

When next I open my eyes, I'm in an American hospital, and Private Berent is at my bedside asking who I am. I tell him, and then I ask a favor.

Write to my father, please. Write and tell him I'm alive.

I WENT HOME . . .
I DID NOT

"Did heaven look on and would not take their part?"
—*Macbeth,* Act IV, Scene 3

AFTER THIRTY-FOUR YEARS, I journeyed home four and a half thousand miles to the capital of the country of my birth. There were only two hundred miles more to travel to the town where I was born, drank mother's milk, went to school, played with friends, laughed, cried, grew up. Two hundred more unflyable, unswimmable, unwalkable, unbearable miles.

I did not go. I was paralyzed by my emotions. They would not stretch one more inch. They stopped dead on Dohany Utca, in Budapest, in the center of a lovely city on Friday night in May in the Dohany Temple.

The temple is giant. Before Hitler, on Friday nights, it was filled with thousands of Jews praying to a God that did not remember the location in 1944–45. Now, the worshipers would have filled no more than a small hall, and that only because the American tourists were there. Otherwise, a small room would have been ample to accommodate the few worshipers whom God spared—and forsook—in the Holocaust.

The rabbi's voice boomed in the enormous temple. The Americans wept. The Budapestians stood erect, or stooped, but did not weep. I heard my soul rattle beneath the outer layer of my body. I wanted to shriek, but instead, I heard myself whisper to the lady sitting next to me: "Were you here when it all happened? Are you from Budapest? How did you survive? You see, they took me to Auschwitz, and I don't really know what happened here while I was there. Was not Budapest safer than other parts of the country? Tell me! Please, I want to know."

"I was here. I had special papers. I survived. But my sister—my sister—she was forty years old; she was beautiful. They marched her tied to four hundred other Jews from her building. They marched them naked, in the middle of the night, in the winter, down beautiful Andrássy Út, and they shot them into the Danube.

"And they did that the next day, and the next, and the next."

The Red Danube.

SCENTS AND IMAGES

CLAD IN A SHROUD of billowing gray, accompanied not by music but by a scent, an unbearable scent of burning human flesh, all my kin, my people, dance a dance of death in my skull, in the tortured maze of my memory.

Smoky spirals swirl toward the sky, assaulting the heavens. The Nazis are burning my mother. It is Auschwitz, 1944. It is summer and the heat is intensified by the fire. It is New York, 1988. It is fall and I am sitting in my well-appointed living room. The brilliant colors on my TV set are intensified scenes from Herman Wouk's *War and Remembrance*. Prisoners of Auschwitz are dumping corpses of Jews into an open pit of fire. Rudolf Hoess, the commandant of Auschwitz, is observing the scene, showing his SS comrade in death how it is done.

The flaming Jews number only several hundred. The smell of only a few hundred corpses is intolerable for these two sensitive Aryan supermen. They are pressing large handkerchiefs to their refined noses to block out the stench.

Then the narrator declares that in 1944, when the

Hungarian Jews were brought to Auschwitz, the Nazis burned 24,000 people a day.

Are there handkerchiefs enough on this planet to block out the scent of 24,000 human beings burning every day, to block out the melting down of my mother?

FEAR

IT WAS MAY 8 yesterday, VE Day, for the forty-fifth time. I have been in America that many years.

By some crazy coincidence, I arrived on the day the war ended. Fresh out of Auschwitz, every sinew of my body was saturated with the stench of the crematoriums.

I will never visit Germany, because even the thought of being surrounded by an entire country of Germans floods my emotions, my head, with chaos. I feel I would lose the precious little equilibrium I have labored painstakingly to regain through the past four and a half decades.

But in America, I thought, I could face a few Germans here and there, I could listen to the sounds of the language that always meant horror and death to me.

Where I was imprisoned, that language spilled from the mouths of some kind of creatures who appeared to be of the same species as I—for they had hair and eyes and arms and toes like the rest of us—but inside, in their heads, where the rest of us try to nurture thought and some kind of humanity, they nurtured something that no language can describe.

Forty-five years later, in New York City, I didn't think I would be unraveled by going to a concert with my

American-born husband to listen to some lovely chamber music played by German musicians. The players were young people, hardly adults. All of them were born decades after their elders melted down my mother and sister and almost everybody else in Europe who emerged from a Jewish womb.

The musicians played like angels, beautifully, skillfully, inspiringly. I almost kissed the sounds they made. I was able to forget the sounds their elders had used to torture me. I blocked them out. I listened with sweet delight. I was grateful to Beethoven and Brahms, I was grateful to these young people who were able to make such sounds of beauty.

But then the concert was over, and there was a reception.

And the old Germans were there, and the somewhat less old, but old enough to have been touched by those days. They stood about, with drinks in hand, well attired in American fashion—for they must have been living here—chatting merrily away. In New York, in America, not a single sound could I pick out in English. They all spoke "that" language. As if they were home, in Germany.

Suddenly, very suddenly, I felt as if I was the foreigner, I was the alien. I was losing my cherished Americanism, I was losing my security of being an almost native New Yorker. I was losing my freedom.

I was just one. There were so many of "them."

I felt my whole *free* American being was being altered. I felt a peculiar physical change, something like pain. I was overcome by something I have never felt at a concert —F E A R.

My husband gently ushered me out.

Epilogue
This Time in Paris
by Irving A. Leitner

THE FIRST TIME Isabella and I vacationed in Europe, we had been married only four years. It was 1960, and we left Peter, our one-year-old, in upstate New York with Isabella's older sister. When we returned nearly a month later to retrieve him, he fidgeted and cried for almost an hour before accepting us back as his rightful parents. Instinctively, at the age of one, he knew how to make us feel guilty for abandoning him while we traipsed about the continent. This time, fifteen years later, we took Peter along, as well as his thirteen-year-old brother, Richard.

On that first trip, we had spent a week in Paris, a week in Rome, and ten glorious days skittering about in general—from Cannes on the Riviera to Florence, Venice, Verona, Milan, Zurich, and London. It was exciting, exhilarating, and exhausting, and we lived on the accumulated memories for a decade and a half. Pointedly, we avoided setting foot in any German city and swiftly moved out of earshot whenever we heard German spoken.

Our resolve in 1960 to avoid anything remotely German was tinged with irony, however, for as it turned out, the dearest friend we made on that trip, and the person who guided us daily around Paris, was a middle-aged German woman to whom we had carried a letter of introduction from a mutual friend in the States. But then, Madame D was an expatriate who had left her native land in revulsion during Hitler's ascendancy and had worked in the French resistance movement during World War II.

Madame D walked with us endlessly and tirelessly, conversing softly in fluent English while we avidly absorbed the sights, sounds, and smells of the magnificent streets and boulevards. On our final day in the city, she took us to the old and shabby Jewish quarter, where a shrine had been erected as a memorial to those who had been systematically murdered in the Nazi extermination camps. It was late in the day, and long shadows were falling as we approached the memorial. Madame D and I slackened our pace, but Isabella quickened hers. Suddenly, Isabella broke down and wept uncontrollably. Madame D whispered, "Go to her. Comfort her." I moved swiftly to Isabella's side. The three of us stood there in the gathering darkness, forlornly contemplative —I with my arms about Isabella, Madame D a respectful distance behind. After a while, we simply turned and left.

In Venice, about ten days later, some mysterious impulse drove us once again to seek identification with our roots. We sought out the old ghetto quarter, trod the ancient streets, and walked the Rialto bridge. A vision of Shakespeare's Shylock materialized for me: ". . . many a time and oft / In the Rialto, you have rated me / . . . You call me misbeliever, cut-throat dog, / And spit upon my Jewish gaberdine. . . ."

In Rome, on a Friday evening, we asked a priest to

direct us to a synagogue. He looked at us with incredulity, then, taken with our audacity, led us there himself. He had never visited the area, he confided in halting English, and felt it was as good a time as any to see what a synagogue looked like in the city of churches.

When we arrived, a sprinkling of elderly worshipers were standing about in front of the building. The services had not yet begun, and pleasantries were being exchanged. At the unfamiliar sight of the black-frocked priest and the alien young couple halting before their synagogue, the Roman Jews stopped talking and stared at us with suspicion.

Unable to speak Italian, we asked the priest whether he would explain to the people that we wished them no harm, that we were only visiting. But our request was more than the priest felt comfortable with. He demurred and we understood. He agreed, however, to wait for us while we peeked inside. I then covered my bare head with a rain cap, and Isabella and I walked into the house of worship.

Immediately beyond the outer door, an attendant directed Isabella in Italian to a flight of stairs at the left. Evidently, this was an Orthodox synagogue, and as was customary, men worshiped separately and apart from women. Since we actually had not come to pray, only to "see," Isabella pointed to her watch and said in English, "Just a minute," and raced up the stairs while I proceeded through the doors on the ground floor.

I really don't know what we expected to see, but somehow it felt right that we should be there, even for only a minute. When Isabella met me outside a few moments later, we rejoined the priest, who was waiting patiently on the other side of the street.

"Why didn't you stay to pray?" he asked.

"We're not religious," I said. "We were just curious."

"I was impressed," said the priest. "There were more worshipers here than in many of Rome's churches. A lot of the churches are empty every Sunday."

"Most of the worshipers tonight were old," I said, as though my comment somehow explained the phenomenon.

In London and in Paris in 1975, ancient ghettos and synagogues were quite remote in our minds. Isabella and I wanted to show our sons the sights the two capitals were famous for. We didn't want to be sophisticated. We wanted to gape and gawk and see things perhaps a bit as we remembered them. And so we did, and relished every single moment of it.

This time in Paris, however, we did not see our old German friend Madame D, who was out of town on holiday. But we did see our Turkish friend, Jessica, and her American husband, George, whom we had met in the States some years before. The day before we were to return to New York, we arranged to spend the afternoon visiting the ancient cemetery of Père-Lachaise, where such diverse personalities as Honoré de Balzac, Sarah Bernhardt, Oscar Wilde, and Frédéric Chopin were buried, among the tombs and bones of thousands of other mortals and immortals.

Isabella and I still had not forgotten the visit we had made to a cemetery in Florence back in 1960. It was a Saint's Day then, and the sight of processions of people carrying lighted candles and flowers, wending their way in the soft evening light through the statuary, tombs, and graves, was lodged deeply in our memories. We hoped now in Paris to recapture some of the feelings we had experienced then. We were disappointed, of course, but the visit to Père-Lachaise was not without its special moments.

As we moved along the narrow paths and lanes, we suddenly found ourselves in a relatively new section of the ancient cemetery—Jessica informed us that it was called the martyrs' area—and there, rising hauntingly from the earth, one after the other, was a series of sculptures commemorating the murdered millions of the Nazi concentration camps.

One sculpture, dedicated to the victims of Maidanek, depicted a towering flight of steps on which a child was struggling upward; another, a desolate, faceless figure, recalled the nameless horrors of Auschwitz; a third, with the names of several *Vernichtungslager* chiseled at the base, showed three skeletal figures clawing at the sky.

Until that instant, Isabella and I had managed to dwell on only the joy of our trip—time enough later for current events, current wars, current crises. For the interlude of July 1975, there was to have been no ugly past, no bitter memories—only pleasure and enrichment.

Still, there had been small, disturbing intrusions, reminders of another time, another place. Fifteen years earlier, everywhere we went we had met American tourists by the scores; now the tourists seemed to be mainly Germans or Japanese. It was almost impossible to avoid the Germans. Isabella, for the most part, tried to ignore them. "I don't mind the young ones so much," she said. "They are an innocent generation. It's the older ones . . ."

But now, in a doleful corner of Père-Lachaise, the fragile fantasy we had so carefully nourished was suddenly demolished. Yet this time, unlike 1960, there were no tears, no heart-wrenching tugs, no need for consolation. This time Isabella wanted only a photograph as a personal remembrance. She posed briefly for Peter, and we left the cemetery, Jessica and her husband going their way, and we returning to our hotel.

Since our second day in Paris, we had made it a nightly ritual, before retiring, to spend some time in a modest café near our hotel, to relax, chat, and reconstruct the day's events. With our departure scheduled for the following noon, this was to be our last evening at the Café Cristal. The weather, which had been glorious for most of our trip, had suddenly turned dismal. A light rain was falling, casting a certain moodiness over us as we entered the glass-enclosed terrace.

The unexpected jolt at Père-Lachaise, coupled with the knowledge that our vacation was ending, had had a sobering effect upon us all. Still, we were determined to extract every last bit of experience possible and tuck it away as a joyful memory of Paris. And so we sat down and gave the waiter our orders.

Isabella had just lit one of her short French cigarettes, and four foaming cups of *café au lait* had barely been placed on our table, when all at once a group of ten or twelve tourists, both men and women, streamed through the two terrace doors and out of the rain. Amid much stamping of feet, doffing of hats and coats, and bantering remarks, the newcomers began to move the tables and chairs about so that they could all be together. The problem for them seemed to be our small table, which was centrally located against the terrace wall, preventing them from grouping all the tables on either one side or the other.

Suddenly, a feeling of dismay clutched me, for in a flash I realized that all the men and women were Germans.

"Who do you think they are?" Isabella whispered.

"Danes," I replied, in an effort to shield her from the truth. The irony of this development coming so soon upon the heels of Père-Lachaise seemed almost too much to bear.

The Germans, appearing somewhat exasperated at our presence, finally decided to divide their party into a semicircle. Two men took a table to our left, two to our right, and the remainder shoved their tables together in the open area behind us. Isabella, with her back to the terrace wall, as well as the boys and I, felt literally surrounded.

With growing anxiety, I watched Isabella's face carefully for the first signs of recognition. She was obviously intrigued by all the fuss and commotion. As the man at her elbow glanced in our direction, a broad, red-faced grin expanding his jowls—an apparent overture of friendliness—Isabella suddenly asked, "Danish?"

"*Nein,*" replied the stranger. "*Deutsch. Von München.*"

Isabella reacted as though acid had been hurled in her face. She seemed to shrivel in her seat. She covered her eyes to blot the man out of her sight. An instant later, with head lowered and lids closed tightly, she placed her palms over her ears, trying to block out every sound.

The grin on the red-faced German vanished. With a guttural murmur and a scraping movement, he readjusted his posture. He mumbled something to his companion, and from the corner of my eye, I could see that both were irritated.

I looked at Peter and Richard. Their faces were ashen. I reached out and touched Isabella. She opened her eyes slowly. "It's them," she whispered, tears spilling down her cheeks. "It's them. They're just the right age."

"Let's get out of here," I said. "Let's go." I glanced

around. Each and every German appeared to be in his or her sixties. Isabella was right. They were all "just the right age."

"Any one of them could have been my jailer—especially this one. I had a red-faced *Oberscharführer* who used to grin like that. He used to club people, and whip them, and grin like a hyena with his ugly little teeth."

"Let's go," I whispered urgently. I signaled the waiter for our check. I could sense that the Germans knew something was wrong at our table. They were exchanging half-audible remarks and glancing pointedly in our direction. I had a distinct feeling they thought Isabella was crazy.

At last the waiter brought the check. I had the money ready and stood up immediately. The boys followed suit. But Isabella could not move.

"Come on, Mommy," Peter said.

I extended my arm to help her up. She took it and rose wearily. "They're the ones," she muttered. "They're the ones."

Negotiating our way past the Germans posed a problem, because they had pushed their chairs and tables so close together, but finally we made it through the terrace door and into the rain. We felt the eyes of the Germans following us all the way.

Outside, Isabella took several steps, paused, and then in a rising crescendo of pain began to scream, "Murderers! Murderers! Murderers!" Peter, Richard, and I quickly hurried her off.

About twenty yards from our hotel, Isabella suddenly stopped and clutched her back. "Help me. I can't walk," she said.

The boys and I sprang to her aid to keep her from sinking to the ground. We stood there in a tight cluster without moving. Not a person passed us. The street was deserted. The rain was now falling heavily.

After what seemed an eternity, Isabella said, "I think I can make it."

We walked the final few steps to the hotel and dropped into four separate chairs in the lobby.

"Are you all right, Mommy?" Richard asked.

"I think so, darling," Isabella responded. "I think so." Then, turning to me, she repeated, "They're the ones. There's no doubt about it. They're the ones."

"How can you be so sure?" I asked.

"Did you see that man's face when he said, '*Von München*'—the pride, the gleam in his eyes? He was no Madame D. He never left Germany. He's the typical '*Deutschland über alles*' German, the Nazi murderer. He could be the one who killed my mother."

"You have no proof," I said.

"I don't need any proof. He's from that generation— the Hitler generation. Have you ever heard a German say he knew about the camps? No. And yet they had to know. When I was in Birnbaumel, they used to march us skeletons through the streets every morning and every night to dig tank traps against the Russians. Twice a day the people saw us. Every day. And if you asked them now, not a one would admit it. And this took place in cities and towns all over Germany. Why, the smoke from the crematoriums blew over their homes twenty-four hours a day. The stench alone should have told them what was going on."

"We've got to do something," Peter suddenly said. "We just can't leave it like this. It's too frustrating."

"We can't ever escape them," Isabella said. "Not until that whole generation has died out."

"I'm going to write them a note," Peter said, taking a small pad and a pen from his pocket.

"What kind of note?"

"I don't know—just a note—just something to make them feel guilty." He thought for a moment, and then, in small block letters, he printed three short lines:

AUSCHWITZ

BERGEN-BELSEN

DACHAU

"Good," I said. "If they had anything to do with the camps, this will tell them they were recognized. If they were innocent, it will explain why we left."

"How are you going to deliver it?" Isabella asked.

"I'd like to throw it in their faces," Peter said.

The boys and I rose and headed for the door.

"I'm staying here," Isabella said, "so please hurry back. I'll be worried . . ."

The rain, which had been falling so heavily only a few moments before, had now tapered off to a misty drizzle. The wet terrace windows of the café glistened with shimmering light as we approached. The Germans were still all there. We could see them laughing. Clearly, they were enjoying their Parisian holiday. It made me doubly angry because they had so marred ours.

At the corner, we stopped and watched them from directly across the street. There suddenly seemed to be so many of them—*a whole Nazi army.*

"I don't think I can do it," Peter said haltingly.

"Do you think we should, Dad?" Richard asked.

"Give me the note," I said.

"How are you going to do it?" Peter asked as he handed me the paper.

I didn't answer directly. I was still undecided about

how to proceed but determined that the message be delivered. I folded the note and started across the street. The boys stood in the drizzle and watched me. "Be careful, Dad," I heard Richard say.

As I entered the café, the throaty sounds of German speech assailed my ears. I stepped across the terrace and into the café proper. A semicircular bar confronted me. A lone cashier was standing at a register totaling the day's receipts. On the bar, a small stack of metal trays, the ones the waiters used to carry the checks to diners, caught my eye. I walked to the bar and took a tray from the stack. I placed the note on the tray and returned to the terrace. For a brief moment, I hesitated as the Germans looked up at me. Then, without a word, and as discreetly as a waiter presenting a check, I set the tray before the Germans at the table closest to me. As one of them reached for the note, I casually stepped out the terrace door and walked back to my children.

Afterword to
Saving the Fragments
by Howard Fast

BOTH ISABELLA LEITNER and I have spent all of our lives in the twentieth century. Since I am somewhat older than Mrs. Leitner, my life touches World War I, and it can be said that in all the history of the planet Earth, there has been no period so mindlessly cruel as this twentieth century, so devastating in its disregard for human life and for every symbol of morality that man has painfully acquired through the ages. World Wars I and II took more lives than all the wars preceding them in four thousand years of recorded history. Such acts as the Holocaust, the bombing of Hiroshima and Nagasaki, and the avalanche of death loosed in Vietnam were matched by lesser but no less monstrous acts—for example, the hundred thousand or more put to death by Idi Amin, the forty thousand victims of the death squads in El Salvador, over a million men, women, and children cut down by the lunatic death squads of Indonesia, the endless murders of both body and soul in South Africa—and the murderous religious mania of the Ayatollah Khomeini.

One could go on and on, filling page after page with the infamies indulged in by our so-called modern civilization; nor could one contend that such practices of the

twentieth century are confined to the more backward nations of the earth. Hardly the case: the West has indeed
taught the more backward nations this manner of "civilization." Most of the showy technical achievements of
this century rest on a solid basis of death, and a new
generation is currently being taught by TV screens and
computers that mercy and compassion are as antiquated
as the horse and buggy, and that even the extinction of
the human race is permissible.

Where, then, against this depressing background, does
an Isabella Leitner fit in? To me, her very existence is an
affirmation of life, a song of hope, a clear bright flame
that defies the murderers of mankind. She is the antithesis of all the hatred and destruction that we have lived
through.

Above all, Mrs. Leitner is an innocent. And what exactly is an innocent? Above all and quite naturally, an
innocent is one untouched by guilt. An innocent is one
uncorrupted by malice, evil, or hatred, one who is without guile and who seeks to harm no other. A young girl,
most fittingly described by the above definition, was
taken from her home by a brutal aggressor, thrust into a
concentration camp under the power of the unspeakable
Dr. Mengele, exposed to horrors that words cannot describe, tortured, used, and starved. She was fortunate
enough to survive.

But the fact that Isabella Leitner survived is the lesser
part of her personal miracle; the greater part is that she
survived—not as a destroyed soul, not as a person utterly crushed by suffering, but as a wonderful, open
woman whose delight in life is so pure and enchanting
that it becomes a song of victory over the mindless, the
hate-filled, and the destroyers.

There have been many other books about the Holo-

caust, books that attempted to put into words the un-
thinkable, to define, explain, or bear witness to a crime
unequaled in all the history of the human race. This is as
it should be. As long as mankind exists, the Holocaust
must be remembered, and every attempt to define it and
recall it should be cherished, no matter how painful.

But in this litany, Mrs. Leitner has created something
unique, the memory of an innocent who, among all that
is awful, managed to find, wherever she turned, acts of
love. So is mankind redeemed. So am I deeply in debt to
Mrs. Leitner, for without these acts of love, hope would
be impossible.

This little book is a fragment—as memories are fragments. Isabella Leitner does not attempt to analyze, to
explain, to create historical patterns. She cannot; she was
a young girl, beloved and innocent, and all she sees and
remembers is recalled through the eyes of a young girl.

But the innocence is not without a knifelike edge of
wisdom. To be innocent and foolish would prove nothing and teach nothing. To be innocent and naive would
negate the validity of responses, but to be cynical would
destroy innocence. When, after her hideous experience,
Isabella's father asks her to pray to God, she rejects this.
She has found in man something truer than the myth of a
personal god who savors the smell of burning flesh for
reasons beyond our understanding. If there is a God for
Isabella, it is something far beyond her father's understanding, something defined only by love and compassion and tied entirely into the lives of men and women
who are not Nazis. This is her wisdom. You do not define or judge the human race by the Nazis. People remain
people, and there is something lovely and tender in her
comprehension of people and their needs.

The liberating Russian soldiers are people. They have

acts of kindness and compassion, yet so long without women, they are ready to grab anyone in a skirt, child or adult—and in the next breath Isabella remembers the wonderful Russian woman on the train, her great bubbling pot of food, and her need to feed anyone who is hungry. She loves all who love. This is her path back into the arms of the human race, and the medley of people of all races who fought and were victimized by the Nazis yet survived fills her with endless delight. Only the Nazi is separate in her mind. For him, there is neither pity nor any shred of tolerance; he must be remembered for all time as the face of evil.

The fragments that you, the reader, have shared in this book are a preachment, a sermon on the wonder and goodness and value of life. All is possible if men and women deal in trust and love. With hatred and suspicion, all will perish. This is the essence and teaching of Isabella's fragments of memory.

Lager Language

By Isabella Leitner,
edited with the assistance of Ruth Zerner,
Lehman College

I will probably never know what prompted me to record these words, actually write this whole account, in my native Hungarian tongue almost immediately after I arrived in this country in 1945. What I did—and after so many years—I am glad I did.

There is an English language, there is French. There is Russian, also Spanish. There is Hungarian, there is Chinese. According to the Bible, God punished humanity in Babel with a madness of languages, but there is one language even God cannot understand—only we do, those of us who were prisoners in the shadow of the crematoriums. I call it *Lager* language, and each word means a different kind of suffering. *Blockälteste* means the head of one thousand prisoners. *Vertreterin,* her substitute. *Stubendienst,* head of a smaller group. *Stubendienstkapo,* head of the *Stubendienste.* But in reality *Blockäl-*

teste meant animal-like screams and even more ferocious beatings; *Vertreterin* meant kneeling; *Stubendienstkapo,* beating; *Torwache,* kicking; *Zählappell* meant standing at attention for hours, in rain, in mud, in frost, often with high fever. If you made a move you would not have recognized your face from the *Lagerkapo*'s slaps, from the *Arbeitdienst*'s kickings. A *Plus* meant that they might take away your sister into another *Block. Mengele* is selecting there in the afternoon. You are looking for your sister, but she is already up in smoke in the *Kremchy.* (That's the humor, by the way, *"the Kremchy."*) The *Sonderkommando* means that they are terribly tired from burning the people. They would be happy if no more *Transport* came today—they had to burn several thousand since this morning. A *Muselmann* meant that you weigh only about fifty pounds and by the afternoon you will be in the *Kremchy. Grese,* that you'd rather go to the *Krematorium* than get into her hands. *H.K.B.* means that you drag the dead from one camp to another and there you might have a chance to *organize,* the sole meaning of which is a chance to steal. *Lux* is a dog that took a few pieces out of you, but you are still alive. *Wurstappell* means you stand in line for hours and then receive a slice of paper-thin salami. (Was it salami? Real salami? It couldn't have been.) *Pritsch* means that fourteen of us are lying on a lice-filled plank of wood. If the wood breaks—and it was built to break—fourteen of us fall on the next plank, and then twenty-eight of us fall on the bottom fourteen people. They are screaming in Hungarian, they are screaming in Polish, and in whatever language the orders are shouted, you must understand them. *Kontrolle* means that the knife you bought with your slice of bread you are hiding in your shoes because you are not allowed to have anything except the rag you are wearing. *Blocksperre* means that you are not allowed to go to the so-called bathroom, but you are also not allowed to make in your pants and you happened to have diarrhea.

Words we have never known but had to learn, the way in America you have to learn English; in Sweden, Swedish; in *Lagerland, Lagerish.*

These words are not interesting for the outsider; most of them are ordinary words with German origin, somewhat bastardized on the way. They are significant only because this limited number of words became a language. A language in which each word meant suffering, and yet a language on which your survival depended as well. The only language necessary. No other language is meaningful. No other is spoken. These words are heard by the second. Used by the second. For instance, a typical conversation:

The *Läuferin* just came from the *Schreibstube.* There was an *Achtung* at the *Küche,* and because of the *Organisation,* the *Kartoffelkommando* and the *Mistkommando* got a *Meldung,* and the *Schreiberin* said that every *Blockälteste* and every *Vertreterin* will have to go for a *Meldung* in front of *Bruna* and the *Lagerälteste,* and the *Kanadakapo* said that there will be a *Generalappell* and *Selektion* in front of *Drexlerka.* Our *Kapo* has already sent the girls with the *Vertreterin Mittag holen,* but by the time they arrive it will be *Zählappell,* and a couple of *Muselmänner* will hide and then there will be *Durchzählen,* and *Knien* and *Blockdurchzählen,* and the *Stubendienste* will empty the *Kübel* and there will be no *Suppe* left for us and we will have to go *Kaffee holen.*

And beyond these there were curse words galore, and incredible as it may seem, even *Lager* songs.

Lager Lexicon

Abstand!—Stand away!
Abtreten!—Move away!
  Dismissed!
Achtung!—Attention!
Alles heraus!—All out!
Alles in die Zelte!—
  Everybody in the huts!
Anfassen!—Pick up!
Antreten!—Fall in!
Appell in die Zelte!—
  Everybody in the huts for
  roll call!
Appellplatz—assembly point
Aufpassen!—Pay attention!
Aufseherin—Female
  supervisor
Aufstehen!—Get up!
Bajtli—Hungarian word for
  bundle
Block—barracks
Blockälteste—senior barracks
  inmate
Blockreinigung—cleaning
  barracks

Blocksperre—closing of
  barracks
Brot—bread
Brotappell—bread call
Brot holen—to get bread
Disinfektion—disinfection
Drahtwache—fence-wire
  guard
Drexlerka—nickname of a
  top SS woman
Durchfall—diarrhea
Durchzählen—recount (of
  prisoners)
Eintopf—hot pot or stew
Esskommando—food squad
Esswagen—food wagon
Feuerwache—fire guard
Fünferreihe—five in a row
Grese, Irma—name of a
  sadistic SS woman
H.K.B.—work squad
  (Kommando) for hauling
  corpses
Holen—to fetch

Kaffee holen—to get coffee

Kanada—a depository of belongings confiscated from arriving prisoners

Kapo—prisoner who was given authority over other prisoners

Käse—cheese

Käse holen—to get cheese

Knien—kneeling

Kontrolle—control

Kübel—bucket (for soup)

Lager—camp

Lagerälteste—senior camp inmate

Lagerführerin—female camp commander

Lagerkommandant—camp commander

Lagerpolizei—camp police

Lagerstrasse—camp road

Läuferin—female runner

Los!—Get going!

Meldung—message, announcement

Mengele, Dr. Josef—the most notorious SS physician; he conducted experiments on live prisoners and selected prisoners for extermination

Mistkommando—excrement squad

Mittag—lunch

Muselmann—totally emaciated, skeletonized

prisoner (ready for the crematorium)

Oberkapo—head *Kapo*

Obersári—nickname for top SS *Oberscharführer*

Oberscharführer—top official

Organisation; Organizacio— organize; acquire ("steal")

Pass amol auf!—Pay attention! (a warning)

Pellkartoffel—potato boiled in skin

Plus—surplus

Pritsch—plank-bed

Revier—station, hospital

Ruhe!—Quiet!

Ruhetreten!—At ease!

Scheisskommando—shit squad

Scheisskübel—shit bucket

Schonung—consideration, ill

Schreiberin—female clerk

Schreibstube—office of the clerk

Schutzhäftling—prisoner

Selekcio, Selekcja, Selektion, Szelektál—selection of prisoners for life or death

Sonderkommando—special squad (people burners)

Spokój ma być—a Polish command for quiet

Strafe—punishment

Strafkommando—punishment squad

Stubendienst—inmate cleaning orderly

Stubendienstkapo—inmate supervisor of cleaning orderlies

Subri Joska—nickname of a particular guard

Suppe—soup

Szájbetegség—Hungarian word for mouth sores

Tattoo—tattoo

Tee holen—to get tea

Torwache—gate guard

Unterkunft—a sorting place for prisoners' clothing and possessions

Vernichtungslager—annihilation camp

Vertreten—present, represent

Vertreterin—female deputy

Waschraum—lavatory, washroom

Wasser—water

Wasserkommando—water-hauling crew

W.C.—toilet (water closet)

Webereikapo—*Kapo* supervising sewing

Wurst—sausage

Wurstappell—sausage call

Zählappell—roll call

Zelte—huts

Ziegel—brick

About the Authors

ISABELLA (KATZ) LEITNER was born in Kisvárda, Hungary. Her father left for America in 1939 to obtain immigration papers for his wife and six children, who were to follow him. He was not granted the documents in time to save his family, and they became victims of the Holocaust.

Isabella's mother and youngest sister were murdered upon arrival in Auschwitz; her oldest sister perished in Bergen-Belsen.

Isabella and her two remaining sisters were the very first survivors of Auschwitz to set foot in the United States. They arrived on May 8, 1945, the day the war in Europe ended.

Her brother, who also survived, arrived in January 1946.

Isabella's first book, *Fragments of Isabella,* was published in 1978. Her second, *Saving the Fragments,* was published in 1986. *The Big Lie,* her book for children, was published in 1992. *Fragments of Isabella,* read by the author, was produced as an audio cassette by Caedmon in 1986, 1989.

In the waning years of her life, the specter of renewed anti-Semitism around the world prompts her to speak tirelessly and write about history's darkest stain, the Holocaust.

She is a board member and media chairperson of the Juvenile Diabetes Foundation.

IRVING A. LEITNER, an American author and playwright, was the editor of his wife's renowned memoir, *Fragments of Isabella,* and wrote "This Time in Paris," the Epilogue to the book. He also co-authored the sequel, *Saving the Fragments.*

On May 8, 1993, Leitner helped make theatrical history in

Russia when his play *Isabella*, based on *Fragments of Isabella*, had its world premiere on the stage of the Komisarzhevskaya Theater in St. Petersburg, the country's second-largest city. Staged as one of the highlights of Russia's Victory Day celebrations marking the defeat of Nazi Germany in World War II, the play received a tumultuous standing ovation. The occasion marked the first exposure of death camp–related drama to the Russian people, who are largely unfamiliar with the Holocaust.

Leitner has also written books for children, including storybooks, pictorial science books, and a dictionary for young people. His works, among others, include the *Sports Illustrated* Book-of-the-Month Club selection *Baseball: Diamond in the Rough* and the colorful book *"ABC's Wide World of Sports."*

As a playwright, he is the recipient of two Jean Dalrymple Best Playwright Comedy/Drama Awards, for 1986 and 1987.